Jesus, A Question of Identity

Jesus, A Question of Identity

J. L. Houlden

continuum

Continuum International Publishing Group
The Tower Building   15 East 26th Street
11 York Road   New York, NY 10010
London
SE1 7NX

First published by SPCK, 1992

British Library Cataloguing-in-Publication Data
A catalogue record for this book is available from the British Library.

Library of Congress Cataloguing-in-Publication Data
A catalog record for this book is available from the Library of Congress.

ISBN 0–8264–8941–9 (paperback)

Printed and bound in Great Britain by MPG Books Limited, Cornwall

Contents

For Alan and Christine Race

Preface

This book grew out of lectures given to students at King's College, London, as part of their work for the Associateship of the College. This course, taken by large numbers of non-specialists, is by far the best established and most widely cast net of adult education in Christian theology in the country. Like the lectures, the book is intended for people without a great deal of specialist knowledge of the subject who wish to understand more about Jesus as a historical figure and as the object of devotion and faith. It avoids technical terms and tries to communicate often complex matters simply but fairly.

Philip Law, then of SPCK, creative publisher, is to be thanked for asking for the book; Richard Harries and Reginald Askew, successive Deans of King's, for asking for the lectures; and hundreds of students for listening to them and thereby helping the author to bring them to greater clarity. I owe a special debt to Graham Stanton and Maurice Wiles for reading the typescript and offering helpful advice.

I also thank Mrs M. Hudson of the Witt Library at the Courtauld Institute and Professor George Steiner for putting me on the track of a depiction of Jesus for which the artist used himself as model. That by Dürer, which provides the cover for this book, is one of many that could have been used. The reader will not have to go far into the book before seeing its appropriateness. Picturing Jesus and forming beliefs about him are always on a knife-edge. Both artist and theologian may so conduct their work, 'at once hubristic and pious' (George Steiner, *Real Presences*, London, Faber and Faber, 1989, p. 208), as to claim, in effect, 'alternate divinity'. And what the believer sees as the wonder of divine incarnation seems to the unbeliever the height of idolatry or of absurdity. As for the believer, the painting serves both to warn of the risk of travesty and to confirm faith in 'Christ in you, the hope of glory.'

Readers keen to explore any aspects of this book in more detail may like to read and browse in *Jesus*, ed. Houlden, London, Continuum, 2005, an encyclopedia with a wide range of contributors.

CHAPTER ONE

Questions about Jesus

WHAT SORT OF BOOK IS THIS?

This is not the first book to be written about Jesus; nor, doubtless, is it the last. Among all the books about him, where does this one stand? It is not a book of propaganda. That is, it is not so keen to convince its readers of a particular view that it plays down all contrary ideas. It is not a book of Christian instruction, saying what should be believed about Jesus by people who count themselves Christians. Nor is it quite a dispassionate academic book. That is, it does not simply lay out its material neutrally, 'for the record'. The writer is a Christian, and he wants to achieve a certain style of shaping the vast range of ideas and beliefs which people have held about Jesus. So it is best described as an explanatory book.

It has two aspects, one historical and the other theological. It sets out something of what can be known about Jesus as a historical figure and of what has been thought and believed about him. It is also concerned with the question of how we may and should think about him now. The question of what we are to make of Jesus is ultimately part of the question of what we are to make of God. For were it not for what may be called the divine 'linkage', Jesus would be an interesting but relatively insignificant figure from a distant and alien time. The inescapable questions are whether and in what ways that linkage, so overwhelmingly important down the years, still has force.

The method is partly chronological. We begin at the beginning of Christian faith and we end at the present day, going from what people first thought about Jesus to what people now think. At the same time, the approach is cumulative and the treatment somewhat repetitive: certain crucial matters keep appearing, in a variety of contexts. Reading will sometimes feel like driving round a partly-known city and being surprised to come across familiar streets from a new angle. The experience can bring relief, delight and illumination. It is certainly a good way of becoming surer of the ground and of fitting things together.

HOW TO USE THIS BOOK

This book, which seeks to inform and also to shape understanding in a particular way, needs co-operation from its readers: they must not adopt the attitude of blotting-paper to ink. The co-operation takes the form of holding together two different and contrary standpoints. They can be labelled *external* and *internal*. Both are laid upon us in our culture in relation to this subject. Yet it is undoubtedly hard to feel equally at home with both. It is more natural for us to stand *either* outside *or* inside the circle of faith and form our thoughts accordingly.

The need to achieve both standpoints applies to believers and non-believers alike, though in different ways. First, the internal standpoint. If we are to understand what it means to hold beliefs about Jesus and to have faith in him, we must step inside the circle. This can be done most obviously by conviction, less obviously and less easily by an effort of sympathy. There must be at least a willingness to enter into issues not immediately important to oneself and to feel how and why people can be passionate about them, sometimes to the point of dying for them. Conviction is not necessarily a total advantage in achieving this internal standpoint; nor is the absence of it necessarily a hindrance. The believer may well see his or her own beliefs – or way of believing – with blinding clarity. That will not always make it possible to enter into other believers' ways of holding their convictions about Jesus, whether now or in the past. And the non-believer may learn, by imaginative sympathy, a wider ability to see what it would be like to feel deeply about this or that issue and to live in the light of belief of this or that character. There is no call for believers to jump to the conclusion that the internal stance is easy for them, or for non-believers to feel it is beyond them.

Secondly, with regard to the external standpoint. The ideal of the dispassionate examination of evidence about beliefs and the objects of belief is too deeply embedded now in Western culture for it to be ignored or wished away – whether or not you approve of it or see its great value. That means that in order to achieve the kind of integrity of mind valued (though rarely achieved) in our society, we need to stand outside our convictions and subject them to universally respected criteria of truth. The evidence must be heard.

In relation to matters of religious faith, many people find this virtually impossible. Believers often think they are letting their side down if they entertain evidence that counts against their beliefs. Non-believers often think religious matters are not susceptible of rational discussion but are matters of 'blind faith' which one either possesses or lacks. Too often, it is believers who have given this impression to their non-believing friends. They would be wise to reflect on whether it is sensible to identify their existing perception of religious truth with the fulness of that truth; on God's being beyond our glimpses of truth about him; and on the many different ways in which truth, of which he is the ultimate source, can reach us. In other words, there are good religious reasons for learning to adopt an external standpoint to matters of religion, however sacred they may be to us.

To sum up this point, here are two quotations to illustrate the two standpoints we have been discussing:

Internal. 'I have been crucified with Christ; it is no longer I who live, but Christ who lives in me; and the life I now live in the flesh I live by faith in the Son of God, who loved me and gave himself for me.' So wrote Paul the apostle in Galatians 2.20.

External. Jesus was 'a famous Galilean held by his followers to be the divine founder of the Church'. So wrote Geza Vermes, a prominent modern student of the world in which Christianity began. We need to enter into both ways of looking at our subject, if we wish to take advantage of the resources of our culture and to do justice to what can now be known about Jesus and about belief in him.

AN EXPOSED POSITION

In taking up the subject of belief concerning Jesus, we are examining Christian thought at one of its central and most exposed points. It is central in that there can be no strictly *Christian* theology without the figure of Jesus and without an account of belief in him in relation to belief in God. It is true that Christianity has always held many beliefs which are not related to Jesus and which sometimes provide points of contact with other religions. But at a deep level, all Christian belief is coloured by belief in and about Jesus. For example, it is possible to discuss and to hold belief in the existence of God without reference to Jesus. But when, speedily, discussion goes on to give body to this belief by speaking about the character of God, then Christian belief in God soon turns out to be seeing him as 'Jesus shaped' or 'Jesus coloured'. And if we are thinking of Christian origins, it is not far short of the truth to say that the distinctiveness of the new faith in relation to its Jewish roots and to its first context lay solely in its adherence to Jesus and in what that adherence meant.

If the central point of the new Christian belief was to do with Jesus, that meant that it involved taking a view about things that had happened. It might also involve abstract ideas, but these had to make sense in relation to Jesus as a historical figure and to historical events. So it has always been with Christian belief, from the beginning until the present day. But beliefs that relate to events are open to critical examination in a different way from beliefs that are purely abstract. There are nowadays highly refined ways of investigating the past in order to sift the evidence for alleged events and their significance. The past that relates to Jesus has been subjected to such investigation with increasing rigour over the past two or three centuries, and in principle has been exposed to it in one way or another from the start. Putting these points in another way, we can say that Christian beliefs have always been dependent on Jesus, and those beliefs have always involved interpretations of what happened to him and what he did; for example, of his birth, his death, and his resurrection.

Over the greater part of Christian history, 'what happened' has been largely a matter of broad agreement: it was there to be read about in the Gospels. True, there were difficulties and discrepancies, but these were mostly seen as on the edges of the story and there were ways (some more satisfactory than others) of accounting for them. They could mainly be put behind one. To a very remarkable degree, the same was true, over the greater part of Christian history, of 'what to believe'. True, there was an initial period, lasting four or five hundred years, when there was variety of belief and controversy over what to believe about Jesus, but after that, for the great majority of Christians, official belief on this subject has been astonishingly stable. As we shall see, there have been considerable shifts in the manner of believing – what belief felt like and how it was expressed – but for many centuries official statements of belief had little difficulty in containing these movements of thought and sensibility. In all this, history and belief were thoroughly interlocked. Few voices sought to separate them, or to question the one in the light of new ideas about the other.

However, since the seventeenth century, both history and belief have been questioned on the grand scale. Later parts of this book will be devoted to some account of why this scrutiny arose and some of the forms it has taken. But at this stage it is helpful to provide a brief answer to the question: What factors brought about this questioning?

1. The broadest factor was a growing willingness to bring allegedly neutral investigation to bear on areas where the Bible (and the Church backing it up) had formerly been felt to be both informative and authoritative. This happened piecemeal; in astronomy, then in geography, then in history. Then eventually principles came to be elaborated which made human reason independent of authority. The pronouncements of the Church

then appeared as one voice among others – all of them subject to scientific investigation, to the weighing of the evidence.

2. Within this general outlook, the new independence of historical enquiry was of the greatest importance for traditional Christian belief. Human integrity now seemed to demand that the biblical story be subjected to neutral investigation. Its importance in the religion of Europe meant that it was (and is still) subjected to this investigation with greater intensity than any comparable set of historical data. But it was not simply a matter of lining up evidence. It was also a matter of the development of an ever-sharper sense of 'the pastness of the past'; that is, a sense of the differences of outlook, customs and ideas between one historical period and another, and of the differences between all of them and the present. Though in one way people had always known this with regard to the biblical past, it had been largely overshadowed by a sense of the biblical record as divinely authorized words on pages, oracles of God, speaking always to the present. Now awareness shifted from the pages to the world (indeed, the various 'worlds') behind the pages: the world of the patriarchs, that of David, or of the prophets, or of Jesus and the early Church. It was a matter of ever-growing sensitivity to the past in its own right. So Jesus became an object of enquiry among all others.

In due course, the same has come to be true of the history of thought and beliefs about Jesus: they too may be seen in the light of the cultural contexts in which they developed. What had at the time seemed simply the 'right' way of expressing belief now came to be seen as the way arising naturally out of a particular historical, cultural context. In this panoramic perspective, beliefs lose their former static quality, and the faith moves from something simply 'given' to something built up in various Christian contexts.

Though this growth of sensitivity to the past was crucial, the new style of attention to evidence was also important – and often painful. 'Facts' and 'beliefs' came to seem much less mutually supportive than had always been supposed. Some of the events surrounding Jesus were revealed as obscure.

In the light of increased scepticism about miracles, many of them came to seem either difficult or frankly incredible. Patching could be attempted (e.g. at the feeding of the five thousand, what 'really' happened was that people shared their packed lunches and the holy presence of Jesus made it seem in retrospect an amazing deed on his part); but the old garment of faith went on falling apart.

3. As far as traditional belief was concerned, an important factor was the widespread abandonment during the eighteenth and nineteenth centuries of the Greek (fundamentally Platonist) philosophical structure in terms of which classic Christian doctrine about God and about the person of Christ had been formulated. This meant that traditional statements about him (such as his being 'of one substance with the Father' and 'one person in two natures') came to seem not so much wrong as alien and forbidding. This style of language had lost its vitality. Such statements were like beached whales: impressive but hard to deal with; just venerable formulas.

4. Such formulas were also a casualty as psychological awareness came to be more popular. This linked up with the growing historical awareness to make it inevitable for people to think what it would have been like to grow up as one who was both divine and human – and to find it hard.

Of course, much of this has left large tracts of official church life and the beliefs of many Christian people largely unaffected. It is a striking feature of Christian history (and indeed the history of many other long-standing elements of human life) that the arrival of the new does not banish the old. The two sit side by side, many not noticing how oddly they fit together, others tolerating their combined presence for motives of varying commendability. All the same, the arrival of the new has played its part in the decline of the attractiveness of Christian belief, including belief about Jesus, in modern times, in much of the Western world. Whether that 'needed' to happen and on what terms belief about Jesus can remain fit and well, are issues that will occupy us in the final chapter of this book.

But because history and belief have been so interlocked over the greater part of the Christian era, because Jesus was not just '*a* Galilean prophet' but one who set off a tradition of fervent and unceasing response and so transcended his own time, the question of Jesus has undoubtedly come to the fore and been the focus of major effort in scholarship and (less so) in church life. 'The question of Jesus' divides into questions such as these: What can we really know about him as a historical figure? What, on this basis, can we believe about him? What is believing in him to be like now? These questions will never be far from the surface in this book.

VARIETIES OF BELIEF

Throughout this book we shall be increasingly aware of people's propensity to create the Jesus who embodies their own aspirations. Simply because he is admired and believed in, he is constantly remoulded in order to be acceptable. The higher the faith, the stronger the tendency to distort, for much is at stake. Though this way of putting it makes it sound culpable, the fact is that it often happens innocently and unconsciously – and, as we shall see, in a certain sense inevitably: we cannot help intruding ourselves into the picture we form and see, in this matter as in all others. Jaroslav Pelikan's *Jesus Through the Centuries* (New Haven and London, Yale University Press, 1985) in its eighteen chapters gives a vivid picture of eighteen different ways in which Jesus has been regarded and believed in, and comes nowhere near exhausting the possibilities (nor, incidentally, does the book wonder what we may then make of all this variety). In a famous image, George Tyrrell (writing in 1909) pictured the Protestant scholar, Harnack, looking down the deep well of history in the hope of discerning the face of the historical Jesus, while all he in fact saw was 'the reflexion of a liberal Protestant face'. But the same is true, in principle, of believers in Jesus and thinkers about Jesus in every age. No one is in a position to claim immunity. The fact of the diversity of perception of Jesus certainly sharpens up our question and injects caution in answering it: What are we *now* to make of

Jesus, both as a historical figure and as involved with belief?

Just consider, by way of sampling, the following range of presentations of Jesus, all of them vivid and deeply important to many believers – and we may be thankful to be brought down to earth by Vermes' 'a Galilean prophet'. There is Jesus depicted like the pagan deity Hermes, the beardless young shepherd, in a third-century catacomb; Jesus the youthful philosopher in a fourth-century statue; Jesus the cosmic emperor, legitimator of Constantine and his many successors in Christian empires down to recent times, presiding in mosaics and coloured glass over numberless great churches; Jesus the creator of the universe, 'God from God, light from light . . . by whom all things were made', in the Nicene Creed; Jesus the enterprising American full of the spirit of 'Go west, young man', who seeks to 'develop and utilize the productive capacity of the people to the maximum . . . economizing human energy . . . eliminating every form of waste . . . The episode of the barren fig-tree is a clear lesson in the conservation of land'[1]; Jesus the champion of the poor and liberator of the oppressed in the political struggles of South America; Jesus the feminist pioneer who blessed the woman who anointed him.

So the final reflection of this chapter, to be placed in the mental 'pending' tray, is: Is it possible for us to identify the 'truth' concerning Jesus, for both history and for belief, engaging but not improperly intruding ourselves? With that question at the back of our minds, we turn now to the start of the story[2].

Notes

1 Quoted in H. J. Cadbury, *The Peril of Modernizing Jesus* (London SPCK, 1962), p.121.
2 It is worth explaining a matter of vocabulary. Almost always in this book, its subject is referred to as 'Jesus', rather than, for example, 'Christ' or 'the Lord'. This is because I wish to keep the reader's attention on the historical figure who inspired the beliefs I describe. 'Christ' began as one title for Jesus among many, representing one strand of early belief (p.18). But it soon lost, for many, its special sense and became virtually an alternative name for Jesus, either

alone or in combination with Jesus ('Jesus Christ') – as it has remained in much ordinary usage. In recent times, it has again acquired deliberate use, as a scholars' shorthand for Jesus as the present object of faith or the heavenly one, with 'Jesus' referring to the historical figure: we read of 'the Christ of faith' or 'the preached Christ' as distinct from 'the Jesus of history'. A reason for avoiding the term here is that sometimes it seems to be used to save us the trouble of ensuring that belief claims about Jesus will stand up in the cool light of Jesus as a historical figure. It can conceal the plastic surgery which belief and enthusiasm unwittingly perform on the face of Jesus. In other words, to those who have an eye on the role in belief of the history concerning Jesus, 'Christ' is an amber light, warning of danger ahead. Also, I have mostly avoided 'Christology', preferring 'belief about Jesus': the former indicates a technical, intellectual or institutional level of belief and thought, and I have wished to range more widely.

CHAPTER TWO

The Beginning of Belief: Paul the Apostle

FAITH COMES FIRST

Modern people who want to know about Jesus are likely to be interested first of all in the events of his life. Their question is: What really happened? Only then are they going to turn to beliefs about him, and the question will be: Do the events support the beliefs? Or will the beliefs stand up in the light of what we can know of the events? It is true that people may be strongly attracted by Jesus, even come to believe *in* him, without knowing a great deal about the events, and it may be their faith which then prompts them to wish to know more. All the same, when it comes to wanting to know *about* Jesus, that is to the stage of enquiry, the order is likely to be as stated above: first the events, then the beliefs.

It may then come as something of a surprise, almost an embarrassment, to recognize that the earliest observable Christianity and the earliest statements about Jesus are in the form of belief rather than history in the modern sense. Though it includes reference to events, that earliest record comes in the form of beliefs about the events. It is history interpreted. In this sense, theology takes precedence over history in the Christian story. And if this prompts modern readers to turn away or feel that they are losing their footing, we ask them to persevere. Though we begin by laying out the early 'interpreted history', we shall then ask what history lay behind the belief. At that point, there will be an attempt at a neutral account of 'the facts', in a modern way, making the hesitant reader feel on firm ground again.

The early interpreted history of Jesus is to be found in the

New Testament, that collection of early Christian writings dating from the hundred years or so after the lifetime of Jesus and largely brought together as a collection (though with significant exceptions) by the end of the second century AD. It takes two main forms: the letters of Paul and the four Gospels. It may be thought strange to include both under the heading of interpreted history: surely the Gospels are records of events? So they are, but they are certainly written from the standpoint of faith. For their writers, this 'history' is not recounted neutrally or dispassionately, but in order to foster faith – as one of them says explicitly (John 20.30–1). So, though there are questions whether any history can ever be written neutrally (the writer is always selective and always has a point of view), there are plainly degrees of neutrality; and the writers of the Gospels make no attempt at it in the modern sense of the term (though Luke makes serious gestures towards the methods of history writing current in his day). Like Paul, their history comes with interpretation from the standpoint of faith. In the case of Paul, however, there can be no question: belief is primary, reference to the events of Jesus' life is meagre (though not negligible). And, almost certainly, Paul was dead before any of the Gospels was written. No doubt much or even all of the information they contain was in circulation, but the interpreted histories which are the Gospels, each containing some of that information and presenting it in a particular way, only came on the scene later, probably in the last thirty years of the first century. Paul died in the sixties. So if Paul comes first, then the priority given to belief in our enquiry is wholly justifiable, indeed inevitable.

Before we turn to Paul's beliefs about Jesus, one further remark is in order. It may seem that in this book the attention given to these first witnesses to Jesus whose writings are still with us is out of proportion. There are two answers: first, while these writers have been viewed in innumerable different ways, they have been omnipresent in subsequent Christian thought about Jesus and their influence has been incalculable. Secondly, in their attitudes can be seen the seeds of whole ways of thinking about Jesus which have persisted throughout Christian history. As well as being influences, they constitute 'types' of Christian reflection and spirituality – and the two roles mingle. As we proceed, the reader may feel: Ah yes, I see Paul's (or Mark's) emphases coming to the fore.

Their way of presenting Jesus, whether in letter or in Gospel, has a merit which is salutary in the light of later developments. We shall find that in later times belief about Jesus often came to be stated in terms of such abstraction that the human story recedes from view or that the heart is not easily engaged: theology seems to have pushed both history and religious devotion into the wings. In these early writers it is not so: what we find ourselves distinguishing as 'history', 'doctrine' and 'devotion' are happily blended; or at least their writings are likely to prompt from us responses in all three areas, and encourage us not to push the three too far apart.

PAUL THE EARLIEST WITNESS

There were Christians before Paul; indeed, before his conversion, they had been the object of his attacks. But Paul is the first to have left direct evidence of his ideas. Jesus himself left no writings whatsoever. Paul's evidence concerning Jesus is in his letters. Some of those ascribed to him are questionable in their authenticity, but there is little argument about the following: Romans, 1 and 2 Corinthians, Galatians, Philippians, 1 Thessalonians, and Philemon. For our present purpose, this list is adequate.

From the point of view of our interest in history and belief with regard to Jesus, a reading of these letters immediately raises two issues. First, we are struck by how little he tells us about Jesus' life and teaching. We may speculate: If all we had was Paul's letters, would there be enough to be a basis for Christian faith? The answer may be Yes, but Jesus would be a shadowy, abstract figure, and his role in Christianity would have been enormously impoverished at the imaginative level. More factually, if all we had was Paul's letters, we should know that Jesus was a Jew, 'born of a woman' (Gal. 4.4), that he died, that he was raised from the dead and then appeared to a large number of his followers (1 Cor. 15. 3–8). About the course of his life, all we should have is the story of the last supper (1 Cor. 11.23–5) – and we may note that it is told by Paul in a form which he has inherited and which reappears in not very different words in the Gospel of Mark written probably almost twenty years later. Of Jesus' teaching virtually all we should have is a prohibition of divorce (1 Cor. 7.10) and an instruction for the payment of Christian missionaries (1 Cor. 9.14) – neither fundamental, and both actually modified in practice by Paul. It is, to our minds, a strange situation. Whatever else Paul may have believed about Jesus, it was certainly not tied to the detailed course of his earthly life or to his teaching. It is possible that parts of Paul's ethical teaching do in fact derive from that teaching, but even so it is significant that it does not seem important to Paul to ascribe them to Jesus. Again, whatever Jesus' significance for Paul, it is not that of an omnibus authority in matters of ethics.

Secondly, we are likely to ask: If Paul, our first available witness, was not in at the start of the Christian movement, how much of what he believed goes back to the beginning and to what degree was he an innovator? Is there substance in the claim sometimes made, that Paul was the real inventor of Christianity? If we put that in the form, 'Jesus preached the Kingdom of God, Paul preached Jesus', there is indeed some substance in it, though 'inventor' gives too much credit to Paul. Supposing that (in this context) we define Christianity as 'response to Jesus', then Jesus elicited it rather than held it himself: others, including Paul in due course, did the responding. If we put it in the form, 'Jesus was a Jewish reformer, Paul made him the centre of a faith', then again, though it gives too much credit to Paul and implies a weak answer to the hard question of Jesus' sense of his own place in God's purposes, the statement has truth in it. He, more than anyone known to us, first articulated, with great clarity, a view of Jesus which placed him at the heart of belief concerning God, and in that way altered the 'shape' of belief concerning God and all else. If, however, the suggestion is that Paul owed nothing to predecessors, then he gives the lie to it (Gal. 1.18; 1 Cor. 15.3). Moreover, Paul like them saw Jesus as the centre of that 'new age' which Jesus had preached. With his lack of attention to Jesus as a historical figure, Paul is uncompromisingly theological in his approach to Jesus; that is, he is concerned with what Jesus signified in God's purposes and with what should be believed about him – or, even more sharply, what it means to believe in him.

PAUL'S BELIEF ABOUT JESUS

Paul's belief in[1] Jesus stemmed from and always rested in what is usually referred to as his 'Damascus road experience'. (The expression has passed into ordinary speech to mean experiences which serve as major turning-points in life.) The story is told in Acts 9, 22 and 26 (in slightly different forms); but Acts was written towards the end of the first century. Closer to the event, which probably happened about AD 35, and from Paul's own hand, we have his statement in Gal. 1.15–16: 'it pleased God . . . to reveal his son in me'. Whatever form that experience precisely took, its effect on Paul was total and permanent. He himself can write of the change in terms of transformation. There is no need here to decide whether it is better to describe the experience as a 'call' or a 'conversion': it has something of both. And it is impossible to do more than speculate about the exact character of that experience or what brought it about. All we know is that Paul had been a keen persecutor of the Christian movement (Gal. 1.13), and his experience turned him into its fervent advocate. Had there been long inner struggle rooted in guilt about his attacking of such a one as he knew Jesus to have been? We do not know. What we do know is that the change in Paul centred on Jesus himself rather than on, for example, dissatisfaction of a theoretical kind with various aspects of his existing Judaism. Such dissatisfaction followed, but there is no clear evidence that it contributed to the change in Paul.

So everything centred on new belief in Jesus. But that meant beliefs about Jesus, for this was no blind, contentless attachment. So what did Paul believe about Jesus? In summary terms, he saw him as God's gift or agent both to Israel and to humankind in general for realizing God's purpose of salvation, and for overcoming all obstacles that stood in its way; and now he reigned as heavenly Lord, soon to consummate that purpose, returning to his faithful followers on earth.

In putting flesh on those bare bones, we find that Paul was not starting from scratch in holding these or other beliefs about Jesus. For one thing, he was not among the first Christians and avows his debt to those who preceded him (1 Cor. 15.3). For another, both he and they saw Jesus in terms of some of their already existing beliefs as Jews, and, for all his great novelty, as slotting into certain aspects of a picture they already possessed. In that sense, at the start Christianity was a new movement within Judaism (in its own eyes, it *was* Judaism!); though its centring on the figure of Jesus meant that it emerged by the end of the first century as a force which Judaism could not contain and which proved radically at variance with rabbinic Judaism as it was then establishing itself. It is probable that already as a Jew Paul had a wide sense of the scope of God's saving purpose – it extended not only to Israel but to at any rate some part of the rest of the human race – and a hope that this purpose would speedily be fulfilled. It is likely that he saw the God-given Law of Judaism (in effect, the comprehensive map for a life well-pleasing to God) as the instrument whose use would be central to the saving process. It may also be that part of Paul's hope was that God would send a human agent (a Messiah = *Christos* in Greek) to take a leading role in achieving his purpose. In this context, we may say that Paul became convinced, as a result of his 'experience', that Jesus was that agent *and* that in occupying that role he carried out the task assigned by Jews to the Law in the purpose of God. Whatever other good uses it may have (e.g. as moral guide, as containing in its books the story of God's dealings with the human race and with Israel), the Law was replaced by Jesus as God's instrument in the business of salvation. On that point, Paul both went beyond most of his Christian contemporaries and put himself radically at variance with Judaism as a whole, whatever its many divisions and differences. Paul states this conviction dramatically: 'Whatever things were gain to me, I count them as dung on account of Christ' (Phil. 3.7). It was the source both of his greatest distress, in that it made him suspect even to many fellow-Christians, and of his supreme achievement, in that it led him to rest his whole mission on the admission of non-Jews to the Church without their having to adopt the key marks of Jewish identity (circumcision, sabbath observance and rules concerning food and meals).

If Jesus had such revolutionary effects for Paul, how exactly did Paul understand the person of Jesus? As we have seen, it was scarcely at all in terms of his human career: Jesus the carpenter or even the prophet of Galilee figures here not at all. This is important not simply as something of a puzzle (How could there be such lack of human interest so soon after the events of Jesus' life?), but also in terms of the story of Christian belief about Jesus. It meant that from the start of Christian writing belief was put in what may strike us as abstract rather than concrete language, or, perhaps better, the use of religious images rather than narrative and human example. It helps to account for the fact that many readers find much of Paul's writing opaque, despite its obvious fervour and immediacy. Plainly (and here most of us must make the effort of sympathy with ways that are foreign to us) Paul was so occupied with Jesus' role in human salvation that the 'human interest' aspect faded from sight; or, it may be, his intellectual pattern-making was such that neither stories about Jesus nor even the teaching of Jesus figured much in its scope.

Paul's conviction that Jesus was God's chief agent for human salvation was crystallized in certain terms used to describe him, terms which functioned as descriptive titles and almost as alternative names for Jesus. Some of them (e.g. Messiah) may also be seen as roles enacted by Jesus. They all exemplify the principle already stated with reference to Paul's general picture: none of these terms is newly invented in order to describe Jesus, all of them existed already in Judaism, but in each case old senses are built upon and new meaning arises by the term's use for Jesus. That is what happens when old words get new applications. We shall find that the route by which the particular term travelled from Jewish use to its new application was different in each case. Partly for this reason, it is unhelpful to think of these terms as logically related to each other and as together building up a rational structure of consistent belief. They are more like a series of poetic images, each shedding its own brilliant light on an object, each demanding appreciation in its own right, but all cumulatively giving a certain impression. All serve to say: Jesus is incomparable, there is no one like him. We take the expressions in turn.

Christ (= Messiah). We have already referred to this term. It is important to see that it had no special position among the terms which Paul used. People often speak as if it did, making statements such as, 'Jesus was the Messiah whom Jews expected'. Modern members of the 'Jews for Jesus' movement in particular have given new currency to such language, and discussion between Jews and Christians is liable to raise the question whether Jesus 'was the Messiah' or not. Such discussion is misconceived. Jesus of Nazareth lived in Galilee in the first years of the first century. 'Messiah' was one of a number of existing images or symbols which his adherents used to express their belief in him as central to the carrying out of God's saving purpose. We shall return to the matter of the status of these images, but it is now important to recognize that Messiah was not the most prominent or creative of them.

All the same, it did play its part – and it raises its own difficulties. For one thing, the expectation of a Messiah was not, it seems, overwhelmingly prominent in the Judaism of Jesus' day, nor did it have a single clear set of associations. This makes it the more surprising that it came to be applied to Jesus, especially as the associations that the term did have were not such as to suit him particularly well. So, first, it is not the case that Judaism was full to the brim with expectation of the Messiah; and, secondly, it is not the case that Jesus was a very suitable candidate to fulfil such messianic expectation as existed. In this light, it is no wonder that it was just one image among many to be applied to him: it simply was not fit to do much of the work of expressing what was believed about Jesus. And if it is pointed out that he was 'qualified' by being descended from David the king and born in David's town of Bethlehem, we have to say that (even supposing these features were not credited to Jesus only after he had come to be seen messianically on other grounds) David had many descendants in Palestine in Jesus' day, just as, by the inevitable process of human propagation, Charles II has many descendants in modern Britain, and many such people may have been born in Bethlehem in the early years of the first century. In other words, Jesus' designation as Messiah depends on other grounds: it was one expression among many of early Christian conviction about him, theological not genealogical in character.

But what was it that could evoke this particular title? There is a persistent theory, which, though often put down, never quite disappears, that Jesus fitted very well the dominant features of 'the Messiah'; that is, he set out to serve God's cause in political and military terms, freeing his people from Roman dominance – and it was for this that he was executed. That led his followers to back-track and create the myth of the pacific Jesus of the Gospels and subsequent Christian belief. This is not the place to discuss the merits and demerits of this assessment: let it suffice to say that the earliest picture of Christian belief, that in Paul's letters, contains not a trace of it. So if that is not the way this title arose, how did it arise? There are two main possibilities. The first is that it came to be applied to Jesus after his resurrection and vindication by God. In so far as the term's existing associations chiefly relate to triumph and victory for God's cause over its opponents, then the conviction of Jesus' victory is a good natural source for belief in him as Messiah; even though this application meant a measure of adjustment to the more conventional use of the term. Though the distinctions involved are by no means as absolute as they seem to us, the Messiah was usually seen in 'this-worldly' terms and his victory in worldly rather than spiritual terms. Neither of these apparent disqualifications need have seemed severe in the light of 'Messiah's' role as only one among a number of titles for Jesus. The other possibility is that from the start the application of this term to Jesus involved irony: despite all appearances (above all, despite his humiliating death by crucifixion), Jesus is God's central chosen agent for carrying out his purposes. It was, in other words, a challenge to normal perception, a defiant banner waved in the face of the world.

This lengthy discussion has been necessary to make Paul's use of the term intelligible. In his usage, it occurs most prominently alongside the name, 'Jesus': 'Jesus Christ' or 'Christ Jesus'; and there is a much discussed question whether already for Paul this has become what it still is, simply a dual name for Jesus, with the technical sense of 'Christ' wholly submerged, or whether each occurrence is a waving of the defiant banner. In favour of the former, it may be that in Gentile circles, for which Paul was chiefly writing, the technical Jewish associations were meaningless, so Paul is not now concerned with them. However, his letters make amply clear that his readers, Gentiles or not, were expected to have a certain repertoire of Jewish knowledge, in particular to appreciate the force of scriptural quotations, and many of them are likely to have been Gentiles formerly associated with synagogues and Jewish religious practices. Sometimes, in any case, Paul does seem to make deliberate use of the term Christ in its technical sense, and one of them points to the ironic interpretation referred to above: 'but we preach Christ crucified' is perhaps better (and certainly more vividly) translated 'we preach a crucified Messiah' (1 Cor. 1.23) – that is, a Messiah wholly different from anybody's picture of that figure.

Son of God. This description was applied to many different persons in the Jewish Scriptures, all in relation to the underlying common image of God as a great king, with his extensive household existing at a number of levels, in heaven and on earth. Thus 'sons of God' included angels (Job 38.7; cf. Luke 20.36), kings of Israel (2 Sam. 7.14), Israel as a whole (Hos. 11.1), and holy, righteous persons (Wisd. of Sol. 2.15). Paul is well aware of this diversity, using the term for Israel as a people specially chosen by God (Rom.

9.4) and for Christians as God's specially devoted servants (Gal. 3.26).

Primarily, however, he uses it as a term for Jesus. But in the light of the wider usage, the question that arises is: How did he manage to narrow it down to Jesus, and how did he understand his special use of it for him? There is some rather uncertain evidence that, as a result of its scriptural application to Jewish kings, it had become a way of designating the Messiah. In that case, we may say that it was an image which had a measure of overlap with 'Messiah'; only a measure, because this association does not exhaust its function in Paul. Another source probably lay in one powerful scriptural story, the subject in this period of considerable reflective attention in Judaism, that of Abraham's near-sacrifice of his precious son, Isaac, in Genesis 22. Paul alludes to it in the language of Romans 8.32: as Abraham at great cost offered his son Isaac to death, so God had offered Jesus – in each case for ends seen as wholly worthwhile. This comparison both brought forward (or helped to bring forward) the term 'son of God', and also showed that Jesus' death was an integral part of his role as God's son, and not some ghastly disaster rendering void any saving purpose. There is no sign at all in Paul that stories of Jesus' birth contributed to his use of the term or that he knew anything about them. They come on the scene only in the Gospels of Matthew and Luke, some years after Paul's death.

Paul's use of the term 'son of God' for both Jesus and Christians is not quite a matter of distinct senses, comparable to the various meanings we listed from the Old Testament. It looks as if the two were seen by Paul as related. Passages like Gal. 3.26 and Rom. 8.14–17 indicate that the relationship granted to Christians as God's 'sons' or 'children' depends on Jesus' role as 'son'. They are as it were satellites dependent on him for their new-found status. Yet the dependence need not be emphasized: 'if children, then heirs; heirs of God, fellow-heirs with Christ'. It is a term which, taken alone, offers the highest position to believers in relation to God, even above the angels (1 Cor. 6.3) – so great is the gift which Jesus mediates.

Lord. From the wide distribution of reference to it in the New Testament writers, it seems that the roots of the Christian application to Jesus of the term 'lord' lie in appeal to Psalm 110.1. This statement served both to legitimate Jesus' heavenly triumph and to guarantee his ultimate cosmic victory. Paul probably makes reference to it in 1 Cor. 15.25. But this was only one strand, though it launched the term confidently into Christian usage. A respected holy person could be addressed as 'lord', and this sense may be dominant in the early Aramaic prayer quoted by Paul in 1 Cor. 16.22: 'Our lord, come'; though allusion to the final clause of Ps. 110.1 is at least as likely. Pagan deities or semi-divine heroes could be called 'lords', and Paul knows this usage: *they* have many 'lords', *we* have one, Jesus Christ (1 Cor. 8.6). Finally, in the reading of Greek versions of the Jewish Scriptures, 'lord' was used for the unsayable name of God. Paul, without comment, quotes statements where this is the case, yet applies them clearly to Jesus (Rom. 10.13). It is impossible to say whether he quotes them, regardless of context, as sheer God-given words which back up his meaning, or intends to put Jesus into God's shoes. We note that modern interpreters distinguish these strands; Paul shows not the slightest sign of doing so. Nor does he show awareness of using a number of complementary images to contribute to a single christological purpose. The images simply appear as appropriate to his argument, but without discussion of their function in a wider way.

Adam. Paul's use of the image of Adam for Jesus' role illustrates this well. It does not serve exactly as a title, more clearly as an image. It works superbly to demonstrate Paul's belief that Jesus' significance is not simply for Jews but for the human race as a whole. He does have a role as son of Abraham (Rom. 4; Gal. 3–4), but he is also second Adam; and this both validates and necessitates the redundancy of Jewish identity as far as God's people now are concerned (Rom. 5.12–21; 1 Cor. 15.22; probably Phil. 2.5–11).

Wisdom of God. Judaism had an old but still live myth which personified God's wisdom as a female consort at his side, working notably in the creation of the world (Prov. 8.22–31). It was a way of expressing the conviction that, despite some appearances, the world is not a random, irrational affair, but the result of wise divine planning. In line with his sense of Jesus' utterly comprehensive role in the execution of God's purpose, and determined to leave no corner of God's work unaffected by him, Paul occasionally seems (it is not wholly clear) to identify Jesus with this figure: 1 Cor. 1.24; perhaps as an ingredient in Phil. 2.5–11; probably in Col. 1.15–20, but this letter is perhaps not by Paul. Whether Paul used it or not, this image most certainly had a great future ahead (p.74).

As we said at the beginning, belief about Jesus did not consist simply in the titles or images which have been described. For Paul, the validating of that belief lay in his inner experience of call and conversion. It was thus inextricably bound up with his own task as a missionary of the good news of Jesus. In so far as he looked back to Jesus, his belief focused on Jesus' death as a martyr, like prophets before him, at the hands of fellow-Jews (1 Thess. 2.14). Jesus who had suffered this fate would certainly return in triumph to save his followers from the terrors of the coming universal crisis (1 Thess. 1.9–10). Paul expressed these basic convictions in the earliest of his letters, and they stayed with him throughout, whatever elaboration they came to receive. Jesus was for Paul the source of what he knew to be his fresh well-being in relation to God. Spiritual enemies had been defeated and need no longer be feared (Rom. 8.35–9), and God had brought to an end alienation and hostility between himself and his creation (2 Cor. 5.17–19). It was as if everything had started afresh.

So it was not at all the case that Christian belief about Jesus started small and tentatively, then gradually built up as confidence grew. We see it beginning in Paul with explosive force. It already gave to Jesus the most comprehensive of roles as God's agent towards the world, from start to finish. Only at the End would his task be complete. Then he would hand over his authority to God who had authorized him and who would then be 'all in all' (1 Cor. 15.28).

Note

1 'Belief *in*' and 'belief *about*' of course represent distinct (but complex) concepts. But 'belief in' only comes to communicable expression in 'belief(s) about'.

CHAPTER THREE

The Beginning of Belief: the Gospels

BELIEF THROUGH NARRATIVE

Paul expressed his faith through the medium of letters, using language that often strikes us, at this distance of time and culture, as alien and difficult. The Gospels are a great deal more accessible to us. We read their stories and for the most part we find them easy to understand; in fact, we are likely to think them rather simple as stories go. But simplicity can deceive. These too are writings of that same distant and varied culture, and we need to make an effort to get inside their world. More important to our concern, these too are expressions of belief, presenting Jesus at two levels – in history and in the beliefs of his followers. Only now it is belief through the medium of narrative: once more, interpreted history.

As we have seen, there is nothing special about that: all history writing, however 'objective' it sets out to be, involves interpretation, at least in the sense of the author's point of view. All the same, there is wide variety in the degree of freedom authors feel in relation to the historical evidence before them; and in different cultural settings different degrees of freedom are acceptable, even natural. By comparison with the highest standards of modern historians, the writers of the Gospels, in line with their setting and the factors involved in their work, exercised a considerable degree of what we should call freedom. Notice, for a start, the ease with which a particular evangelist feels able to alter and adapt a predecessor's work in accordance with his own point of view. Modern students of the Gospels differ considerably in their assessment of the extent of this freedom with 'the facts', in effect their assessment of the accuracy and trustworthiness of the Gospels from a historical point of view. We shall return to that issue in the next chapter. Meanwhile, we simply take note of it as we turn our attention to the evangelists as authors, Christian authors at that, out to communicate their belief about Jesus.

Authors have individuality. Perhaps the greatest achievement of recent study of the Gospels has been to demonstrate and describe the individual outlooks of the four Gospels with a clarity never seen before, or, perhaps, not since the immediate time and place of their first appearance, presumably among people who understood their authors' minds. Each writer has his own way of believing, his own message to communicate; no doubt much affected by those around him, for we cannot but believe that Christian communities of those early days were pretty tight-knit affairs. The evangelists were not like modern writers, shut away in their East Anglian cottage to get the job done, any more than they were like modern archivists just reproducing the records. They were authors who were in a measure spokesmen for their Christian groups, and in part critics of those groups, in the way that pastors always try to improve as well as represent those in their care. We now give a sketch of each evangelist's way of believing in Jesus, bringing out its distinctive features. Each in his own way recounts the past, but in the light of his present belief in Jesus, now the heavenly Lord. We begin with the Gospel of Mark, almost certainly the first of the four to be written, let us say about AD 70. We place ourselves at that astonishing moment in the development of Christian belief when, about forty years (all that time) after Jesus' lifetime, it first occurred to some otherwise unknown literate Christian that he must put his faith down in telling the story of the one who had transformed and now dominated his world.

THE GOSPEL OF MARK

It is relatively straightforward to outline Mark's way of believing by listing the chief terms he uses to identify Jesus, as we did in the case of Paul. It is much harder, but perhaps more important, to describe his overall sense of Jesus. There we meet surprises and some bafflement. We begin with the easier task.

We need to realize that there was no centrally organized body of beliefs, no 'bank' of authorized words to be used in all Christian congregations. Each had its own favourite terms and used them with its special nuances of meaning. Nevertheless there were overlap and sharing, and Mark has many terms in common with Paul, so much so that, for this and other reasons, it is sometimes suggested that this author had been affected by Paul's teaching and had picked up many of his emphases.

So, in Mark's account, Jesus was certainly Messiah (Christ), and it is stated at three prominent moments in the story: the very beginning (1.1), a formal recognition by the disciple Peter (8.29), and by Jesus himself in reply to the high priest at his interrogation (14.62). However, Mark never says what he thinks it means – Has it just become a stock way of referring to Jesus? – and there are signs that he thought it too vague, even misleading, if left on its own. He also makes something of Jesus' Davidic descent, probably seeing that as carrying messianic force (10.47–8; perhaps 2.25; 11.10); but again there are signs that it will not do just as it stands: 12.35–7. 'Son of David' Jesus may be, but it cannot be left at that.

Jesus was also 'son of God', and Mark probably saw this as closer to the heart of the matter. Use of it 'brackets' his entire story, and occurs also at crucial moments within it. After its appearance in the opening words, it forms the heart of the divine authentication of Jesus at the baptism (1.11): with this status, son of God, Jesus is the focus of God's opening up of communication with us – heaven is split open and the voice is heard. The words ('Thou art my beloved son') come mostly from Psalm 2.7, perhaps already carrying messianic overtones (symbols overlapping) or perhaps simply being striking scriptural words now seen as prophecy fulfilled. 'Beloved', here and in the comparable mid-way scene of transfiguration (9.7) and again in the parable in 12.1–12, may allude to the story of Abraham's offering of Isaac for death. We saw Paul's reference to it, and constantly, in the Greek version of it, which Mark would have known, Isaac is described by this word. If this is so, then Mark depicts Jesus' baptism as already being his dedication for death in God's cause.

The same term, 'son of God', is used to voice the executioner–centurion's faith at the end, in 15.39. That faith is created by the sight of Jesus' death. As God's son, Jesus is meant to die, and it is his dying that shows him to be God's son. Beyond the possible allusions to messianic ideas and the Isaac story, we have no clear clues to Mark's exact rationale in using this title for Jesus. Like 'Christ', it had perhaps already become in large measure simply a way of referring to Jesus, a sort of alternative name; though it is unlikely that that is the whole of the story. Like Paul, Mark gives no ground for thinking that this term is related to stories of Jesus' birth. Perhaps we should see it in partly functional, partly relational, terms: Jesus is God's utterly special agent.

As far as the term 'lord' is concerned, so prominent in Paul and apparently in a slogan current in his circle (1 Cor. 12.3), Mark makes almost nothing of it; its only 'freestanding' occurrence as a term for Jesus is in 11.3.

Mark does, however, bring to the fore a term for Jesus which Paul had never used at all and perhaps did not know: 'son of man'. Moreover, Mark probably saw it as the most precise and useful way of all for designating Jesus. Maybe precise for Mark, but certainly obscure for us. More ink (much of it erring or inconclusive ink) has been spilt over the question of how to understand this expression than over almost any other matter of New Testament interpretation. This is not the place to be other than bold (and rash) in stating a view which may have a chance of coinciding at some points with what Mark had in mind. Luckily that is all that concerns us here – questions of background and of the term's senses in Jesus' spoken Aramaic can be left aside.

'Son of man' seems to have served Mark well to express exactly his perception of Jesus. Just as Psalm 110.1 (see in the discussion of Paul on p.22) shed floods of light on the applicability of the term 'lord' to Jesus, and perhaps Psalm 2.7 did the same for 'son of God', so Daniel 7.13 legitimated, even seemed to compel, the use of 'son of man'. That scriptural passage refers to a symbolic figure, 'one like to a son of man', who represents the martyrs of Israel now vindicated by God, for whose cause they had died, and who is central in executing his ultimate purposes. He is a representative, almost ideal, figure for God's faithful people. The expression 'son of man' is a Hebrew–Aramaic idiom, at its simplest, for 'man'; so the Daniel passage refers to 'one in human form', corresponding to the animal symbols used earlier to represent other peoples in the visions which the book recounts. What Mark seizes on is a set of three features of the symbol: God-given authority, suffering, and vindication by God. For the element of authority, see 2.10 and 2.28; for suffering, 8.31; 10.45, etc.; for vindication, 8.38; 14.62, etc. Jesus is the one who, possessing God's full authority, must suffer, and then is assured of God's vindication. He is central in his purposes for the world. The vital 'work' which this term does is to 'explain' the necessity of Jesus's suffering. It was a task of supreme usefulness in early Christian faith, where Jesus' triumph in resurrection could, as it were, be assumed, but where his death could be an embarrassment (cf. 1 Cor. 1. 18–24). Mark grasped this idiomatic phrase from Daniel's Aramaic, turning it into Greek, where it no longer had idiomatic force; and it became, naturally, a title for Jesus: he was '*the* son of man'. (Compare: in Iran, *ayatollah* is an ordinary term for a religious leader in Islam, and they are many; in English, the term being alien, '*the* ayatollah' normally became the designation of one man, Khomeini.)

These titles do not exhaust the meaning of Jesus in Mark's faith. For Mark, Jesus is unquestionably the one from God, come to carry out his saving purpose: notice his abrupt entry on the scene at the start of the story – from Nazareth, yes (1.9; 6.1–6), but in effect 'from God'. He acts throughout with urgency, moving dramatically towards the death which is the climax of his role. He preaches the rule of God (1.13–14), exemplifying it in word and deed, and he is a seer privy to the secrets of its future consummation (13); but his death is, overwhelmingly, the goal of his journey. Compared with that giving of his life as 'a ransom for many' (10.45), even his resurrection is barely stated, opening a door towards the future (16.6–7).[1] But the death is what has to be grasped –

in all its starkness which is represented without mitigation, or almost so (see 14.3–9). The words of Jesus from the cross, expressing abandonment by God (15.34), face us with that most sharply. Mark's Jesus is awesome, forbidding, and greatly mysterious; like the righteous sufferer in Psalm 22 who, for Mark, illuminates Jesus' role. He leaves those around him puzzled, uncomprehending and treacherous. Questions are left hanging, even for us who can read the whole story as Mark has given it to us (8.21). Jesus attracts divine fascination and is an enigma whose depths we may not cease to explore. At the same time there is great assurance that, through all this bafflement and reversal of human values (8.34–5; 10.35–45), there is a future of great splendour, hardly won (4.1–20, 26–9; 13.26). Mark expressed a courageous faith, blinking no human realities, achieving no cheap assurance, yet wholly assured all the same.

THE GOSPEL OF MATTHEW

The writer of what is probably the second of thhhe Gospels in order of writing incorporated almost the whole of his predecessor's work and added in his own extensive material. All the same, he felt free to make adjustments and alterations to Mark, some of them small but still significant. He did this to express his own vision of things, including his way of perceiving Jesus.

As far as formal terms are concerned, he is content to use virtually the same ones as Mark (though 11.19 may show a trace of the application of 'wisdom' to Jesus such as we found in Paul, p.23). However, Matthew sharpens up their sense, as one may sharpen up an image being projected on to a screen.

Thus, Matthew is glad to demonstrate how Jesus fulfilled messianic prophecies to the very letter (2.5–6). And, again showing a liking for being specific, he roots Jesus' sonship of God in a virginal conception – an amazing God-produced birth, comparable to the births of great scriptural figures like Jesus' ancestor Isaac (1.2), though in this case the mother is probably seen as remarkable because under rather than over the age of motherhood (Genesis 21). This sonship, interpreted by way of

Isaiah 7.14, gives Jesus a slogan-like title, 'God-with-us', later reiterated but in terms of *Jesus'* presence with his own (18.20; 28.20).

Matthew leans towards the specific. He leans also towards a firm sense of Jesus' total authority and triumph (28.17), and in particular stresses the vindication aspect of 'son of man', notably in the extended picture of his universal judging of the human race (25.31–46). Jesus has huge resources of power, kept behind the scenes in his lifetime (26.53). Matthew is particularly struck by this paradox of great messianic power concealed by meekness, and gives scriptural warrant for it, from Isaiah (42.1–4; cf. Matt. 12.17–21) and Zechariah (9.9; cf. Matt. 21.5). It is this paradox that impressed Matthew, rather more than that of life-only-through-death which held Mark's attention. He also holds together Jesus' great beneficence (11.28–30) and extreme severity (22.11–14; 25.41). Towards both friends and enemies, Jesus is the very model of an oriental potentate; and Matthew's sense of justice is of a kind that sees in this both what is right and proper *and* the way to exercise authority (over his own Christian congregation?).

But it is in his belief in Jesus as messianic teacher that we have Matthew's most striking contribution. Again, we may surely see here Matthew's sense of the needs of his people. It is true that Mark uses the actual words 'teach', 'teaching', 'teacher' more often than Matthew. Nevertheless, Matthew gives a great deal more practical guidance for everyday Christian life, whether it concerns aspirations and rules for basic morality (5; 6.19–7.14) or religious practice (6.1–18), for missionary activity (10) or church discipline (18), or else the hope and fear with which to approach the undoubted coming End when Jesus' authority will no longer be concealed at all (24–25).

As in Paul and Mark, we find again that belief about Jesus is expressed by way of a number of complementary images and by way of an overall picture. There are contributions from both inherited tradition about Jesus and from Matthew's own needs. Like his predecessors, Matthew believes in Jesus as he *needs* to believe in him. As in all such cases, it is a measure of the greatness of devotion that so much is projected on to its object. One can be cool and merely 'accurate' about those who do not evoke a deep reaction. Except in part by noting the ways in which he adapts Mark, we cannot precisely draw the line in Matthew (or any of the others) between good, reliable tradition and construction on the basis of needs; though scholars put forward their more or less reasonable ideas. There are certainly aspects of Jesus as presented here which may not have initially appealed to Matthew's predispositions; and in them an authentic voice calls through to us powerfully. The charismatic prophet who can say to prospective followers, 'Let the dead bury their dead' (8.22), works clean contrary to Matthew's concern for traditional law (5.17–19; 23.3,23) and for decent order. However much Matthew has presented 'his' Jesus, it is far from the case that without any restraint he has manipulated him to his own purposes and wholly moulded him according to his preferred pattern. We shall meet this phenomenon, one way or another, time and again, in its ambiguity, so hard to define.

THE GOSPEL OF LUKE

Luke, like Matthew, makes use of Mark, and perhaps of Matthew too, certainly of other material, much of which is also found in Matthew. So it is not surprising that he too shares Mark's terms for expressing belief about Jesus. Only, unlike the others, he makes much use of 'the Lord' as a way of referring to Jesus (e.g. 10.1, 41). Presumably it was a way of speaking common in Luke's circle, as it still is in many Christian groups. We cannot tell exactly what overtones it carried for Luke, but we know he was aware of Psalm 110.1, the great text for validating it in early Christian scriptural theology (cf. p.22): he quotes it in Acts 2.34 as well as Luke 20.42.

It is also true that 'lordship' characterizes what Luke believed about Jesus' present role. He sees the ascension to heaven, permanent in its effects and looking forward only to his eventual return to earth, as the goal of Jesus' career – his entry 'into glory' (24.26; cf. Acts 1. 1–11). The events recounted so proudly in Acts, recording the ever-widening spread of the

Christian message about Jesus, are all done under the aegis of the heavenly Jesus. Everything is empowered by 'the spirit', but Jesus himself intervenes audibly at crucial moments (Acts 9. 4–5, 10): for the Christians, heaven and earth are never out of touch.

Luke also has a liking for another term with a great future ahead in Christian usage, one not used by either Mark or Matthew and, apart from the Pastoral Epistles (1 and 2 Timothy and Titus), not common in early Christian writings: 'saviour' (2.11) – a term that was used of God in the Jewish Scriptures (as also in Luke 1.47) and that pagans also used of their deities. As in the case of 'lord', its wide currency meant that it carried the idea: 'you have your saviours, but Jesus is ours – and really does save' (cf. 7.50). So these terms had their polemical aspect in addition to affirming and reassuring faith.

Jesus' arrival as Messiah (and son and lord and saviour) into the midst of Israel is seen more warmly by Luke than by his fellow evangelists. Though of course he is aware of the terrible rejection of him by at least the leaders of the Jews, he regards it with as much sadness as judgement (e.g. 23.28–31), and makes plain the strong continuity between old Israel and Jesus as God's gift to it. So Jesus comes to the temple in Jerusalem as to his rightful place, in infancy and childhood (1–2) and in his teaching ministry (19.45–21.38) – a cue faithfully picked up by his followers (24.53; Acts 2.46; 21). Mary and the rest who surround Jesus' birth (1–2) breathe a welcoming Jewish air, and, even more than in Matthew, his birth as 'son of God' (1.35) recalls God-given births in the Old Testament.

From the point of view of what later came to be thought of as 'doctrine' about Jesus, Luke seems to have made little distinctive contribution. But on a wider understanding, we can see that Luke's belief concerning him focused on Jesus' inspiring and attractive moral and spiritual example. The message is quite simple: give yourself generously – to God in constant prayer (3.21; 9.29; 11.1–4); to people, with the generosity of God himself (7.36–50; 10.25–37; 15.1–32); and to both even in the face of cruel death (23.43,46). Jesus dies as a faithful martyr, and Luke's sense of this may have been illuminated by Wisdom of Solomon 2.1–3.9. Notice the 'righteous one' in Wisd. 2.15; Luke 23.47; Acts 7.52. (Many of these passages involve alterations of the Marcan prototype at significant points.) This is an edifying and moving style of belief about Jesus, evoking peace and love, and it has echoed down the ages, if more in the spheres of art and devotion than of technical statements of beliefs.

THE GOSPEL OF JOHN

'The Fourth Gospel' has always been seen as set apart from the others: after all, the other three have much material in common, this one shares little. And it is distinctive in other ways: its inclusion of few stories and long discourses, often appended to them; its omission of episodes important in the others, such as the temptation and the transfiguration of Jesus, and of exorcisms and (almost) of parables. But from the point of view of our present concern, there is, initially little cause to see it as odd man out. John happily employs the terms expressing belief in and about Jesus (they are both confessional and descriptive) that we have found elsewhere: lord, son of man, saviour (once, 4.42), Messiah and son of God. He may have seen the last two as virtually synonymous, and he certainly regarded them as fundamental, combining them in his formal statement of purpose in 20.30–1 (and 11.27). The 'Father-Son' relation may indeed be seen as carrying the whole structure; and 'Son' now applies to Jesus uniquely, established so in Christian usage. (Unlike Paul, Matthew and Luke, he carefully uses another word, 'children', when referring to Christians in their relationship to God.) In that sense, this Gospel gives the impression of representing more deliberate planning as regards belief about Jesus than the others. So this writer too draws on the stock of Jewish resources for speaking of agents of God, but gives them new turns of meaning resulting from their application to Jesus of Nazareth.

Some 'new turns' in this Gospel occur partly as a result of inherited expressions being set alongside terms scarcely found elsewhere in the New Testament; and all contribute to the total picture. The first involves the term 'the prophet' (1.21; 6.14). This may testify to the inclusion of the belief that Jesus fulfilled a form of expectation that was favoured among the Samaritans and based on Deuteronomy 18.15 (see also Acts 7.37).

Much more important, especially in view of what lay ahead, was another special way of referring to Jesus: he is 'God'. Three times John used this language: in 1.1, 1.18 and 20.28. (In the second reference there is a measure of doubt, in terms of early manuscripts, whether he wrote 'God' or 'son'; there was a difference of only one letter in the Greek abbreviation probably used.) In all three cases, there is both identification between Jesus and God, and a noting of differentiation between them. In 1.1, the words 'with God' make the latter point; in 1.18 the adjective 'only-begotten' (or 'uniquely derivative'); in the last case 20.17 ranges Jesus with his followers as distinct from God ('my God and your God') before one of them makes the identification in v.28. So the way of using the term is not straightforward, to say the least. What may John have had in mind?

We shall return to this subject; let it now suffice to say that it is inappropriate to look in John's setting for high metaphysical sophistication such as came later to surround this belief. We are in one of the many kinds of Jewish thought then prevalent, adapting itself, perhaps very adventurously, to speech about Jesus, who is, for the author, the one who has opened the way to God as no other has (14.6). In other words, we should look for exactly the same kind of development we have found in relation to the other terms for Jesus: Jewish imagery, scriptural texts, then movement of sense as a result of the new application. But is the claim here made for Jesus at all out of line with the others? Does it leap ahead, especially against a background of Jewish monotheism which it was surely unthinkable to breach? Is it a piece of wholly novel revelation, a bolt from the blue?

Two aspects of Jewish thinking contribute particularly to the statements before us, one of them belonging to the world of religious metaphor or symbol, the other secular in context. We have discussed the powerful Jewish use of the symbol of 'wisdom' (p.23), suggesting the universality of divine order. In some Jewish circles, the symbol of God's 'word' had come to play a comparable part. We find it in Psalm 33.6, and already half-personified in Isaiah 55.10–11. It lies behind the creation story in Genesis 1, where God 'speaks' and creation occurs. It figures, now personified, in the Wisdom of Solomon (9.1; 18.14–15), and the prominent Jewish thinker, Philo, active in Alexandria at the time of Jesus, had made extensive and speculative use of it. Again it was personified and seen at work in, even identified with, heroes in God's service such as Moses. And because it was God's 'word' which (who) was thus active, it was a way of speaking of God at work. A text like Exodus 7.1 ('I have made thee a god to Pharaoh') could lead Philo to speak of Moses as almost a representation of God. Now Jesus is God's 'word', not only bearing and speaking but actually *embodying* God's whole plan (1.1, 14).

Alongside this we place Jewish legal practice whereby (in days of slow communication) an agent (e.g. in diplomacy or business) could act as the fully empowered representative of his employer – *as if* he were the man himself; and if he were the man's son, so much the better, the identification was all the stronger. John uses this analogy explicitly in 13.16.[2] And there is strong probability that, combined with 'word' language so prominent in John's prologue, it formed the picture of identity-cum-distinction in 1.1 and the other passages. To see Jesus, God's word and son, is *as good as* seeing God himself (cf. 14.9). The idea of *agency*, found already in Mark 9.47 and Matthew 10.40, is fundamental in shaping this Gospel's whole concept of Jesus as the one sent and authorized by God.

A third style of Jewish thought, this time more speculative in tone, may also have made its contribution. There is some evidence that in some Jewish circles, apocalyptic in general tendency, there was pressure towards 'tampering' with pure monotheism. Thus angelic beings and others might be described in terms that implied a status as representatives or 'locations' of God. It is possible that Johannine Christianity came to birth among sectarian Jews who entertained such ideas. What was new was their application to a human being, active so few years before in Palestine.[3] To us there seems to be a wide gap between the down-to-earth metaphor of 'agency' and the kind of speculation just described. It may not have seemed so strange to these first-century Christians to fuse such different modes of thought. It is of course hard for us to know how much weight to place on the more 'rational' explanations of the 'God-language' in John and how much to put on the more 'extravagant' explanation.

Other strands may also be present: for example, 'lord and god' was an acclamation addressed to the Roman emperor; so 20.28 says, in part (as does the trial scene before Pilate), 'Jesus is my king/emperor/messiah'. What is clear is that we are still in the realm of what *we* might call poetic imagery and metaphor. We are not at this stage called upon to face such questions as, 'If Jesus was God, how was the universe upheld during his time on earth?' or 'How can God be two and yet one?' We are being told rather: Jesus is God-to-us; and further questions are not appropriate. At the same time, the Johannine Christians knew that here lay the chief danger-area, especially in relation to Jews (5.18; 8.59).

Probably it was already implicit in Paul's use of the symbol of wisdom,[4] but the idea of Jesus as 'word' certainly introduced into Christian thought an element which was again to be more important in the future, and has often been a source of difficulty: the idea of Jesus' pre-existence, that is, the idea that before his conception he had long (eternally) existed in heaven (1.1; 8.58). Leaving aside for the moment the difficulties in this idea, let us see it as expressing in yet another way the early Christian conviction that Jesus filled the total 'meaning-space' between God and the human race. For a former Jew whose head contained ideas of eternally existent 'wisdom' and 'word', this conviction was bound to make Jesus step into those roles as into all others.

Indeed, it is possible to see John as – almost – working with a deliberate plan to show how Jesus fills concentric circles of meaning in relation to God and the world; and certainly John achieves a greater concentration of Jewish symbols and images to demonstrate Jesus' significance than any other early

Christian writer. No wonder he was such a fertile source for later theology, even when his language was transposed into other cultural keys than his own.

Thus, at the widest, in relation to the whole created order, Jesus is the agent of creation. 'Word' (1.1–3) shows that; so does the use of symbols with 'I am' (e.g. bread of life, 6.35; light, 9.1), some of them already associated with 'wisdom'. For Judaism (e.g. Ecclus. 24), God's wisdom was crystallized and normatively displayed in the Mosaic Law. Now Jesus steps into its role: 1.17; and again, the 'I am' symbols (e.g. way, 14.6 – Psalm 119.1, 33; light, 9.1 – Psalm 119.105). That Law was centrally obeyed in the worship of the Jerusalem temple. Now Jesus is to be the 'place' where God and humans meet: 2.21; 4.21–3; 7.37–8 in light of Zechariah 13.12. The temple is the scene of the great festivals that bind God to his people. Now Jesus is the authentic lamb of Passover (1.29; 19, where Jesus' death coincides with the ritual slaughter of lambs for the feast and involves allusions to the ritual).

Finally, the absolute use by Jesus of 'I am' (8.28,58) may fortify the idea of 'Jesus in the role of God'. If not exactly turning our attention to the divine name revealed in Exodus 3.14 (where the Greek version does not clearly indicate its being in mind here), it plainly echoes usage in passages like Deuteronomy 32.39 and Isaiah 43.13; 51.12 (the Greek version is clearer than the English), where God asserts his case to the world. Similarly, in John, Jesus in God's stead asserts his claims to the world's allegiance, his sufficiency as the deputy and mediator of God for salvation and judgement. Revealing God, he draws all to himself.

It is no wonder that such a lofty portrayal of Jesus raises the question whether, for John, he truly belongs to this world. 'He is a pre-existent divine being, whose real home is in heaven . . . No doubt he is portrayed as subject to human weaknesses . . . but these in no way diminish the extraordinary control he exercises upon his own fate . . . There is in him no trace of that uncertainty, that helpless sense of being flung into the world which Heidegger, with picturesque concision, calls *Geworfensein*, that incomprehension and bewilderment which ordinary human beings can never entirely escape.[5] As we shall see, that tendency was not uncongenial to those in the subsequent period who made such extensive use of this Gospel over all the others.

All the same, this heavenly figure is identical with Jesus of Nazareth who lives and dies in this world. It is simply that in this Gospel, the two levels of his existence are more thoroughly knitted together than in the other Gospels. In them, God's agent on earth (messiah, son of God, etc.) moves towards his heavenly destination, where, as son of man, he will be vindicated and from where he will return to judge and rule. In this Gospel, his origin too is heavenly, so that origin and destination are one and the same; and his role is unified from beginning to end, with judgement, the discriminating of light from darkness, being his role already in the here and now (1.51; 3.17–19; 5.27). And his return to heaven (exaltation) is, in both language and significance, fused with his death by crucifixion (lifting up), as the use of the ambiguous Greek verb *hupsoō* (12.32) so strikingly shows.

This account of early belief concerning Jesus has not been exhaustive. The Letter to the Hebrews, for example, works out an intricate analogy between Jesus and the role of the Jewish priesthood, in particular the high priest on the Day of Atonement, as laid out in the Jewish Law. There are allusions, clearest in 1 Peter, to the figure of the innocent and redemptive sufferer in God's cause described in Isaiah 53. This passage, subsequently to become one of the most used prophecies of Jesus' role, was probably less important in the writing of the Gospels than used to be thought; still, it may play a part in the formation of the thought of Mark, so often allusive in his use of Scripture, even though the similar imagery of Psalm 22 is more explicit in his work. What we have hoped to demonstrate is the way in which early Christian belief worked, by way of both letter and narrative, with a multiplicity of images and symbols, all contributing to the various portraits of Jesus in which early Christians embodied their faith in him.

Notes

1 The Gospel is taken as ending originally at 16.8.
2 See P. Borgen, 'God's Agent in the Fourth Gospel', in John Ashton, ed., *The Interpretation of John* (London, SPCK, 1986).
3 See John Ashton, *Understanding the Fourth Gospel* (Oxford University Press, 1991), pp.137–59.
4 'Word' and 'wisdom' were virtually interchangeable in some Jewish thought by this time (e.g. Wisd. 9.1), and pre-existence was associated with both.
5 Ashton, ibid, p.239.

CHAPTER FOUR

Jesus and History

HISTORY TO THE FORE

Over the past three centuries, what is called Western culture (though it is also to be found in part in north, south and east) has gradually sharpened its concern with 'objective' or 'neutral' history, the past observed and written about 'for its own sake'. The quotation marks are not meant to signify cynicism but to point to the difficulty and complexity of the task, even to its impossibility: each observer forms his or her own picture. Not that cynicism is wholly out of place. It may seem fraudulent to claim concern for neutral history for a culture existing in a period and place which have seen history forced into servitude to propaganda and ideology with unprecedented efficiency and in which there is every reason for the widespread suspicion of the constructions placed by authority upon events. Despite all this, the claim is justified. Our sensitivity to propaganda, in past or present, witting or unwitting, is itself evidence of it.

We have already seen that no area of the past has been exempt from this determination to discover what really happened. The Bible, as God's word, was long felt to enjoy privilege or exemption. It was a no-go area, first as a whole, then with regard to the New Testament, then (sometimes unintentionally) with regard to Jesus. For many believers, the Bible, in whole or part, is still a no-go area, where neutral historical feet should not intrude, and dispassionate (unbelieving) enquirers have nothing to contribute. It is fenced around, and inside the privileged enclosure, special standards apply. More than anything else, this represents a feeling of impropriety, amounting to sacrilege, in the bringing of a neutral mind to holy things. But it also represents, implicitly, a denial of all-round holiness, including the holiness of enquiry into truth by all available means. That debate remains alive and vigorous. Meanwhile, enquiry into the history surrounding Jesus has proceeded apace, marked by thoroughness, intensity and no lack of conceptual difficulty, resulting from its intricate and varied dance with belief. Later, we shall trace the course of the dance.

The reader attracted to this book by an interest in history may feel let down by its almost total concentration so far on belief. The reason for that initial concentration was explained at the beginning of Chapter 2. Now the question is: What lay behind the belief that so quickly arose? Was there enough in 'the facts' to warrant it, even to compel it? Or was it the fruit of various kinds of delusion, for which perhaps explanations are not hard to find? The reader has every right to be impatient for information leading to an answer to such questions. The massive historical effort of recent centuries has provided a great deal of information and presses it upon us though, as we shall see, much of it is possible rather than probable, probable rather than sure. These things happened so long ago; our sources are limited and not wholly or simply amenable to the kind of enquiry that interests us now; but with care we can discover much, even if we must forgo the luxury of certainty. The limitations that face us face all enquiry into the past, remote or near, to one degree or another. We must not ask the impossible. As we have seen, in the case of Jesus, the history comes to us mediated by way of two powerful factors: first, he was the object of profound belief and devotion; second, with their Jewish background, early Christians found their theological and religious identity not in abstract ideas so much as in Old Testament texts which seemed to them prophetic of Jesus. What was told and believed about Jesus was deeply marked by both factors, the one general, the other detailed and specific in affecting both the statement of belief and the telling of Jesus' story.

HOW CAN WE KNOW ABOUT JESUS?

The obvious source for evidence is the Gospels. No doubt they tell us a great deal about Jesus, but identifying it and weighing it is no easy matter. The Gospels are slanted. They were not written to answer our modern questions, about the order of events, causality and psychological awareness, but to commend faith. Still, however sceptical one is about particular aspects, there can be little doubt about the historical value of certain major thrusts of Jesus' activity and teaching, especially if they differ from attitudes prevailing in the late first-century Christianity that produced the Gospels. This applies to such features as the great concentration in Jesus' preaching on the theme of 'the Kingdom of God', his appeal to the socially unacceptable, and his hedonist reputation. (Mark 1.14–15; Matt. 21.31; 11.19 are passages which typify these features.) All this contributes to a profile of Jesus.

So does knowledge of the place and time in which Jesus lived. The picture of Jesus as rooted in the Jewish environment of his day has been much sharpened in recent years, as knowledge of that environment has grown. However 'unique', a person's identity and public intelligiblity depend on the person's 'fit' in relation to the surrounding culture. So with Jesus there are questions like the following, not always capable of clear, uncontroverted answers: the character of Galilee – how provincial in relation to Jerusalem? how liable to political unrest? how affluent? how Hellenistic in culture? how much divided culturally between town and country? And the character of Judaism – what was the range of tolerated differences on the interpretation of the Mosaic Law? which matters of belief and practice were reckoned particularly sensitive? how important were the so-called 'parties' in Judaism (Pharisees, Essenes, Sadducees), what exactly did they stand for, and how did they relate to one another? While much of the evidence on these matters is as problematic as that of the Gospels, being also the product of a later period, it sometimes offers facts and perspectives different from those of the Gospels. Thus, the intense concern in Jewish circles with the details of incurring ritual uncleanness (e.g. from contact with corpses) and with tithing makes us pause: it is easy for us to underestimate the importance of such matters as we now read the Gospels (cf. Mark 1.40–5; Luke 10.31–2).

Sometimes the external evidence confronts us with startling

gaps in the Gospels. In the time of Jesus' childhood and young manhood, the town of Sepphoris was being rebuilt on the latest, ultra-modern, Greek-culture lines, with Hellenistic architecture, theatre and civic life. It was visible from and very close to Nazareth. It embodied the cultural aspirations of Herod Antipas, ruler of Galilee. Yet it makes no appearance whatsoever in the Gospels. That reminds us of the probable remoteness of their places of composition from the sites of Jesus' life: though, puzzlingly, other evidence points the other way, especially in the Gospel of John (e.g. concerning the pool in John 5 where archaeological work seems to confirm John's topography).

Sepphoris reminds us of the strength of Greek culture in the towns of Galilee in Jesus' time. This makes us recognize the strongly rural and village setting of his life and activity which the Gospels depict. Though towns certainly figure, it is mainly as places visited and left rather than resided in; but even this is not wholly clear. Did Matthew have any evidence that made him alter the reference to Capernaum in Mark 2.1 to 'his own city' (Matt. 9.1)? Or did this Gospel-writer, like the others literate and surely urban, simply assume that Jesus must have had 'his city'? The proximity of Sepphoris to Nazareth also forces us to entertain the unverifiable possibility that Jesus knew some Greek, the language of urban commerce and culture.

This book cannot enter into detailed discussion of all the issues which arise in relation to Jesus' world, though some of them will reappear later in this chapter and elsewhere. My purpose so far has been to stimulate sensitivity to them and indicate their relevance. From the earliest days of critical study of the life of Jesus, they have played their part. For example, Reimarus (whose ground-breaking work was published in 1774–7) used knowledge of messianic, anti-Roman agitation, as well as hints he saw in the Gospels, to depict Jesus as a failed revolutionary whose disciples stole his body and fabricated his resurrection.

There is a third kind of evidence that can contribute to our attempt to form a picture of Jesus. Non-Christian literary references to him are few and mostly of little importance. Those from later Latin writers are brief, and, more than anything else, what they show is the marginal role of the Christian movement in the horizons of most upper-class Roman writers of the late first and early second centuries. The only other literary reference is of more interest and comes, where it might be expected, in the history of Josephus, who was born in Palestine as Christianity was beginning, and wrote in Rome towards the end of the century. His reference to Jesus was subject to inflationary Christian additions, and a probable original version goes: 'At about this time lived Jesus, a wise man. He did astonishing feats. He attracted many Jews and many of the Greeks. Upon indictment brought by leading members of our society, Pilate sentenced him to the cross; but those who had loved him from the very first did not cease to be attached to him. The brotherhood of the Christians, named after him, is still in existence.' If authentic, it is an instance of sympathetic objectivity, at a time when, lower down the social scale, relations between Jews and Christians were far from friendly and reaching breaking-point. It is not clear whether Josephus saw the Christian brotherhood as now outside Judaism; probably not – he certainly says nothing about its separation or exclusion.

PROFILES OF JESUS

Gaining a picture of a historical (or present) figure is a matter both of evidence about events and of arriving at an overall impression. Often a number of different profiles may be put forward as frameworks within which the detailed evidence about events or teaching may be assessed. Where the evidence is not abundant or straightforward, this procedure is all the more likely to be fruitful. At all events, a number of different characterizations of Jesus can be proposed. We shall see how far they take us.

Preacher of the kingdom of God. The image of God as king pervaded the Jewish Scriptures, but there is little to indicate that the phrase 'the kingdom of God' had at this stage achieved wide currency in Judaism. Yet in the first three Gospels, it dominates Jesus' preaching, especially in the parables. (In the Gospel of John, with its pervasive centring of all images on Jesus, it almost disappears (only 3.3,5), to be replaced by Jesus as king, 12.13; 18.33–19.16.)

It signifies the assertion of God's universal and ultimate sovereignty. More than any other term, it places the emphasis of Jesus' message in *eschatology*: that is, it looks with assurance to the dawn of the coming age. We have already seen, in discussing some of the titles used for Jesus, the prevalence of this emphasis both in the Judaism of the period and then in early Christianity. Particularly in the apocalyptic writings (in the Bible, the Book of Daniel and the Revelation of John), we can see how all-absorbing this style of religious conviction could be, filling people's horizons. Its chief features were divine judgement (adverse for God's enemies), the restoration of fortunes and the establishing of harmony and prosperity, in fact the bringing about of a new world (Rev.21.1).

There is little reason to doubt that Jesus' proclamation of the coming age was within the terms of this expectation and that it was marked by excitement, urgency and hope. So much was this the case that there is also no reason to doubt the Gospels' sense that Jesus' healings and other marvellous deeds were signs of God's rule already breaking into present life. So where the kingdom is referred to in 'present' terms (e.g. Matt. 12.28), that is not meant to foster an endorsement of the status quo. It means that radical change is on the way, indeed already to be seen.

Proclaimer of renunciation. No aspect of the Gospels is more likely to cause embarrassment among modern believers (and cynicism about their performance among non-believers) than Jesus' dismissive attitude to family and property. Those who follow him are to renounce both (Mark 1.16–20; 10.17–31). Though there are signs that some Christians continued to live in accordance with these injunctions well after Jesus' lifetime (and ultimately in the monastic movement), the evidence is that very soon most Christians were in urban congregations where such a way of life was in practice impossible. It is not surprising that, in the letters of Paul, all written with urban groups in view, such commands find no place. That means that by the time the Gospels were written, and in the places of their writing, renunciation of these kinds was no longer current general practice, though it may have applied to some Christians. (Thus Matthew's provision of instructions for itinerant, simple-living Christian missionaries in ch. 10 as well as for settled congregations in ch. 18 may well indicate that, in the church life he knew, both elements were present.) The renunciations were therefore soon subject to various kinds and degrees of metaphorical interpretation – as they have mostly been ever since: they depicted vividly a life-style, a degree of commitment to which one should always aspire, or a standard to be sought in the inward self even if it could scarcely be lived out in practice.

Their prominence in the Gospels surely indicates, however, that Jesus, wholly in line with his kingdom preaching, demanded an absolute response, expressed in total attachment to his cause, by way of renunciations that harked back to prophetic examples in the Scriptures. There are parallels in the similarly motivated Jewish community of Qumran revealed in the Dead Sea Scrolls.

Accepter of marginal people. Again, the absence of evidence that the Church of the later first century went out of its way to fill itself with despised and morally rejected groups, offering them unconditional welcome, points to the authenticity of this prominent feature in Jesus' life. The Pastoral Epistles, for example, show how far staid respectability could already dominate Christian life, within a few decades. We have already pointed to passages like Matt. 21.31 as recording the memory of this feature of Jesus' work. Stories like those in Luke 7.36–50 and 19.1–10 bring it vividly before us. Luke's Gospel gives this aspect particular prominence and it doubtless carried practical force (now hard to specify) for him; but it is too widely spread elsewhere to be his invention and witnessing only to some need or pressure in his church.

Critic of the Jewish Law. No side of the Gospels' presentation of Jesus causes more difficulty for interpreters than this. It is partly that no aspect of early Christian life and identity caused more anguish than deciding how one stood in relation to Jewishness and therefore to observance of the Law. This meant that on no matter was there more likelihood that Christian groups would adjust their picture of Jesus to their own views and practical needs. It was a matter on which it was hard to secure consistency even within a particular Christian group – there were tugs in different directions.

Thus, Mark seems to have believed that Jesus was a marginalizer of the Law, as it were a Paul before Paul's time: with regard to sabbath observance (2.27), food laws (7.19), and the overriding importance of love (12.28–34). (This is not the only indication that Mark may have worn Pauline spectacles.) For Mark, it seems, the central urgency of the kingdom pushed all else, including the Jewish past (except for prophecy) and the Jewish way, to the edges. Matthew, on the contrary, saw Jesus as both endorsing and intensifying the Law, and on each of the matters just mentioned he amended Mark to make his view plain. Jesus came of impeccable lineage (1.2–17). Strict sabbath observance might be subject to benign, scripturally backed dispensation, but on no account was it dismissed (11.28–12.14). Food laws were not tampered with and only plain abuses of the Law condemned (15.1–20). The duty of love did not override other commands but pervaded them (22.34–40). All the same, while endorsing the Law for his Christians (5.17–19; 23.3,23) and intensifying its stringency (5.20–48), he was aware that the conditions of the kingdom, proclaimed by Jesus, meant the dawning of new moral demands, scarcely compatible in letter or spirit with the old (8.22). Matthew represents a style of Jewish Christianity which saw Jesus' way as the messianic fulfilment of Jewish hopes and as entailing no abandonment of the God-given Law. Luke too had no wish to abandon this inheritance. Perhaps the compromise arrangements whereby Jews and Gentiles might coexist in the Church and truly fulfil God's promises, recorded in Acts 15.1–29, give the best clue to his attitude, and to the reason for it. We may reasonably suppose that he had the task of uniting Jews and non-Jews in his church, and to that end both affirmed the Jewish inheritance and imposed only limited obedience to the Law on Gentiles (in terms that in themselves symbolized their full acceptance into the re-defined people of God). John, as we saw, largely and comprehensively placed Jesus fairly and squarely in place of the Law, as of all other aspects of God's former ways of disclosing his person and will.

This variety makes it hard to be sure of Jesus' own attitude. Was he Marcan, Matthean, Lucan or Johannine? Or was he none of those? All reflect later situations that were not his at all. Yet, in their very different ways, all four agree that Jesus was a critic of the Law. But could not even that depiction reflect the Jewish–Christian antagonism of the later first century? On that view, it was not so much that, as a matter of history, Jesus was against the Law at all, but that Christians and Jews were later opposed to each other – for a variety of reasons, including the execution and rejection of Jesus, and not least the Christians' devaluing of the Law as their centring on Jesus came to the fore and as the Church became more and more non-Jewish in composition.

Knowledge of contemporary Judaism suggests that in reality Jesus was not beyond the bounds of dispute in relation to the Law, his Jewishness not in question. It was a period when Jewish groups took different views on many matters of observance, even though coexistence rather than toleration would be the better way of describing the atmosphere. It was a time of controversy, in which Jesus represents one strand (hard to identify precisely for the reasons we have indicated). Even supposing he was critical of the Law, as Mark proposes to us, much of his criticism does not go beyond the pale, for example on sabbath or on the primacy of love. On this view, in thinking that Jesus did so place himself in confrontation with Jews around him, Mark mis-estimated the facts. In a realistic view of Jesus in his time, he was a Jew whose attitude to Law observance was given a fresh context, leading to new priorities, by his conviction of the coming new age.

Critic of the temple. Whatever its precise significance (the interpretation of it is different in each of the four Gospels), the incident in the temple (Mark 11.15–17) is widely accepted as historical and plainly betokens hostility to the existing role, and perhaps the Sadducaic management, of the temple. In this, Galilean attitudes to the capital may have played a part; so, surely, did prophets' attacks on the cultic establishment, now seen in the light of the coming new age (cf. Jer. 7).

Martyr for God's cause. Another much controverted question is how far Jesus foresaw his death. Was this his long-accepted destiny, as the Gospels say, or was he taken by surprise and devastated, as the cry in Mark 15.34 has been taken to show? Whatever the right interpretation of the words, 'My God, my God, why hast thou forsaken me?' (Mark's picture of Jesus' utter passivity before God? an allusion to the whole message of Ps. 22, with its climax in vindication?), there is nothing improbable in an intense conviction of prophetic destiny in proclaiming the kingdom including the inevitability and appropriateness of martyrdom. Scriptures, like Psalm 22, were at hand to show how such a death should be seen, as were actual instances, from Maccabean times, two centuries before, onwards, when servants of God's cause met this fate. John the Baptist is a martyr who figures prominently in the Gospels, partly portrayed (especially by Matthew) as a lesser replica of Jesus.

Charismatic leader. This term, taken from the sociology of religion and not from the vocabulary of popular Christianity, has come into prominence to epitomize the historical reality of Jesus. In this 'neutral' perspective, it sums up admirably his character and role. 'Charismatic' describes figures whose effect is to transform the whole outlook of those whom they attract. It may or may not be the case that, from a standpoint of cool assessment, the teaching of such a one is wholly original or his life exemplary. It may be that some single aspect or happening triggers off the effect. Cases differ. It is the effect that counts. In that sense, the precise historical reality remains to be identified, as we have been attempting to do in the case of Jesus. Nevertheless, in arriving at a profile of Jesus, *charismatic leader* will be as good a summary as any. It helps us to see why different early Christians focused on different aspects of Jesus' career as carrying charismatic force: whether his teaching, his death or his triumph.

JESUS AND EVENTS

Understanding the historical realities of Jesus involves not only reaching the most adequate general profile that we can. There is also the question of events. It is no surprise that Christian belief and identity centred on these events, especially Jesus' death and resurrection. Nor should it be any surprise that because of their importance they were the subject of vigorous interpretation. The telling of the stories reflected the various interpretations. Indeed, it was the interpretation of these great episodes that both notably chimed in with and crucially helped to form the four distinct styles of belief about Jesus that we find in the four Gospels. So, as in the case of attitudes to the Law, there is bound to be difficulty in arriving at an exact knowledge of what happened.

That does not mean that we can have no knowledge of what happened. Especially in the case of Jesus' arrest and death, we can use knowledge of probabilities in such cases to gain a reasonably dependable picture. For instance, Jewish–Roman arrangements in Palestine were such that a figure like Jesus, attracting popular support and acting as in the temple incident, would certainly be viewed with alarm by the authorities. Whether or not Jesus was, in anything like our sense, a political figure, he could be felt as a threat to civil and economic stability. It is probable that it was from that angle, rather than from strictly religious objection, that Jewish as well as Roman hostility came. That the Gospels present the matter in religious terms would then reflect Jewish–Christian religious conflict of the later first century. From this starting point, we can go on to see how each of the evangelists has his own way of telling the story, that is his own view of the meaning of Jesus' death. It comes through in such matters as Mark's picture of Jesus' extreme passivity, the victim whom God would vindicate, and of the extreme callousness and brutality of those around him, including his own followers; in Matthew's heightening of the apocalyptic impressiveness of the death and the requital administered to Judas; in Luke's picture of the moral and spiritual serenity of Jesus' death; and in John's exploration of kingship and truth alongside Jesus' role as the 'true' passover lamb.

The resurrection stories present the historian with different problems; though in the Gospels they are all of a piece with the rest, especially with the passion stories. For the modern historian, there is bound to be the divisive question of attitude to the miraculous. Here some will take a positive view, but if so, then because of wider, non-historical factors; others, for philosophical or general historical reasons, will take a negative view. On any showing, the stories reflect different interests, not hard to see as consistent with the tendency of the evangelist who tells them. It is misconceived to try and harmonize them. Yet behind them is the earlier evidence of Paul about resurrection appearances of Jesus in 1 Cor. 15.5–8, taking us close to the time. There are inconsistencies, or at least different tendencies, in these accounts: for example regarding the character of what was believed to have occurred, whether in terms of physicality or of 'inwardness'. The historian may feel constrained to say 'something happened' without being able to say much about it, except in terms of its manifest effects. The historian is unlikely to see adequate basis for conjectures about deliberate deception adopted by Jesus' disciples as a way of getting out of a tough spot. The historian will also note that there were those in early Christianity who saw Jesus' victory in terms of his exaltation by God (i.e. in 'faith' terms) and spoke of no 'event' of resurrection (e.g. 1 Tim. 3.16).

The stories of Jesus' conception and birth, told in the Gospels of Matthew and Luke, again raise somewhat different questions. However, there is once more the general issue of miracle. These stories seem to have arisen only relatively late: earlier sources know nothing of them. Not wholly consistent with each other, both accounts lean heavily (more plainly in the case of Matthew) on scriptural warrant, to the extent that they may seem to be almost wholly dependent on prophetic texts. This is true to a degree of the passion stories, but much more so here. The historian may feel it is impossible to penetrate behind this screen. Once Christian interest turned, for whatever reason, to the subject of Jesus' origins, those who expressed themselves in narrative terms saw Scripture as the key point of entry, whatever tradition was able to contribute. Here interpretation is at its maximum. John chose to deal with this subject in quite other, more abstract terms: Jesus, 'in the beginning . . . with God', came 'from above' and 'dwelt among us'.

Other, lesser events of Jesus' story (e.g. baptism, temptation, transfiguration) similarly exhibit in their telling the emphases of the particular evangelists, and it is hard to establish exactly 'what happened' or whether the stories represent religiously motivated invention. Classes of events, such as healings, are so large that they can scarcely lack historical foundation, though it is probable that both form and details represent work done by faith and devotion. Indeed, we can see the process before our eyes, as an evangelist modifies a story taken over from a predecessor (a minor example being Matthew's doubling of the blind man in Mark 10.46–52, in Matt. 20.29–34, perhaps to heighten the impressiveness of the testimony).

WHAT IT AMOUNTS TO

Resorting now to general terms, we can say that Jesus of Nazareth, in a way not true even of socially comparable figures of his time such as John the Baptist, effected an enlarging of vision and a special confidence directed towards a new future in relation to God and the world. By contrast with much contemporary apocalyptic thinking, Jesus, we may suppose, saw judgement as outshone by salvation.

The historian's assessment has to steer a careful course: between seeing Jesus as so distinctive that he makes no sense in the context of his times and seeing him as so ordinary, so thoroughly part of his background, that the massive and speedy effects of his life become incomprehensible. Two extremes are unlikely: on the one hand, that our accounts of Jesus are wholly shaped by faith and that in reality he was nothing very remarkable; and on the other hand, that the accounts owe nothing to faith and that all happened and was said exactly as told. What is hard is to know at what point between the extremes truth lies. Finally, we cannot tell exactly how great a role the resurrection played in the shaping of the telling of the story as a whole. Must it bear most of the weight in explaining how Jesus, a teacher well within the parameters of Judaism, came to be seen in such lofty and special terms? Or must there have been much about Jesus that was so attractive and unusual that faith was already and understandably present, to be 'boosted' and crystallized by the resurrection experience? Paul inclines us towards the former view, the Gospels towards the latter. Once again, where exactly to place our historian's finger is not a matter likely to produce agreement. But decisions on all these matters are not irrelevant to the different ways in which belief comes to be formed, arising from the events.

In some circumstances indeed attention to the historical picture of Jesus as it is available to us creates a whole new way of believing. Not only does it form a predisposition to give priority to his human situation and characteristics, it also moves the focus away from his person (Who was Jesus?) to his function (What did he stand for and achieve?). Thus it is more widely agreed that Jesus preached the kingdom of God and presented it in terms of forgiveness, joy and restoration than that he preached about himself. That is, while Jesus left an indelible mark as the propagator of certain values and priorities in life, precise accounts of his own person may owe more to later Christian reflection than to his own claims. This way of looking at the matter certainly promotes a style of belief which is very different from that concentration on the defining of Jesus' person which characterized the subsequent centuries. In later terms, the style of belief to which historical study points (Jesus as preacher of the kingdom of God) seems nebulous; but it is hard to deny its power, and it places a question-mark against the long monopoly of the style which succeeded it and which has dominated Christian history. To put it another way: much in the Gospels points away from Jesus himself to God. 'Why do you call me good? no one is good but God alone' (Mark 10.18) symbolizes this strand as well as any other single statement. The strong probability that this feature of the Gospels represents historical authenticity places the later intensity of interest in Jesus' person as something to be defined with all possible precision in an interesting light.

CHAPTER FIVE

Worship and Belief

A CRUCIAL TRANSITION

We have seen some of the chief ways in which early Christians put their beliefs about Jesus into words. We have also seen something of the history relating to Jesus, viewed from a standpoint outside Christian conviction. At the beginning of the last chapter, the question was raised, whether the history was sufficient to support the beliefs, and the question was not answered. Implicitly, you, the reader, were left to decide. Perhaps, in the end, that is the best that can be done. Certainly we should recognize that 'the facts' could never *compel* belief. There is also that elusive ingredient of faith.

Yet even that is not a simple matter. It is not as if faith were an easily identifiable commodity that might be used to tip a balance of possibilities; though sometimes it looks as if that might be the right picture of the situation. In *God Incarnate: Story and Belief* (ed. A. E. Harvey, London, SPCK, 1981), two authors, A. E. Harvey and Geza Vermes, contributed not wholly dissimilar essays (numbers 5 and 6). Both give an account of the historical context of Jesus and of conclusions that may be drawn. The two discussions of the history notice many of the same features; but the former proceeds to a position where belief may properly follow, the latter does not. Faith seems to be the differentiating factor. (Reading the two essays also suggests the perplexing question of what evidence could possibly authorize, let alone demonstrate, that a person be seen as God incarnate, the case being unparalleled.)

Take another contrasting pair. A Muslim, on the basis of the Qu'ran, will hold a belief in the virginal conception and the heavenly ascension of Jesus. Yet no one should claim that the Muslim's faith is thereby Christian. On the other hand, many Christians, staunch in their allegiance, now believe in neither the virginal conception nor the ascension, and others see them as perhaps believable but as having little bearing on Christian faith and certainly not as essential to it. Whether scepticism on these two subjects has to do with a general difficulty over miracles or an understanding of the relevant New Testament stories as deriving less from historical facts than from certain ways of expressing belief, the connection between alleged events and religious commitment is far from straightforward.

Nor should we assume that a certain array of events, listable in advance, is necessary to support a particular belief. If we take the traditional heart of Christian belief about Jesus as his being 'God in human form', the incarnation of God, then it is not clear that any particular set of historical facts is necessary or even conducive to such belief. In the wide spectrum of human religious possibilities, we can imagine (and discover) that in certain circumstances 'incarnation of God' status might be given to figures whose lives had a wide range of characteristics, from the humdrum to the spectacular, the saintly to the immoral. Human religiosity is capable of many different judgements when it comes to identifying the divine. And the more divine status is seen in abstract or otherworldly terms, the less the issue of the characteristics of the human person in question arises. As we shall see, the Christian understanding of divine incarnation has never been wholly unrelated to the particularities of Jesus' career. Indeed, Christians have often seen them as moulding their conception of God. Without the events, Christian belief would have been substantially different in character, even apart from the narrow matter of 'belief in' the events themselves.

The upshot is that a belief in divine incarnation *need* not involve the history relating to Jesus, though in the Christian case obviously it has traditionally done so. On the other hand, the history relating to Jesus cannot *necessitate* the belief that he was God incarnate. Again, however, in the Christian case, the paying of high religious attention (to go no further) to Jesus would have been highly unlikely if he had lived as a blameless village carpenter and died peacefully in his bed. In fact, the events, the stories and the beliefs were thoroughly intertwined from as far back as we can trace, knitted together in tight interpretative patterns, derived chiefly from the Jewish Scriptures.

The division between belief and history, which we have observed in this book and which is pressed on us by modernity, is nowhere clearly discernible in the earliest Christian writings. The move from the history to the belief is invisible to us. Yet in the light of modern perspectives about both history and belief, it cannot fail to interest us. The rest of this chapter will attempt to see the invisible – to identify the join between the career of Jesus and the emergence of belief that can be called distinctively Christian.

JESUS IS GOD

We have already stated baldly that the traditional, distinctive Christian belief about Jesus is that he is the incarnation of God. In the last section, it was a convenient shorthand, a working statement. But there need be no apology, as if to imply that the idea would have been better expressed in some more careful statement; for by the early second century, such language was well established among Christians. There is no question of its having been slowly built up to over centuries of laborious debate. Like Venus from the waves, it seems to appear fully grown (though we shall see that the truth is more complex). What is the evidence?

Pliny. Like British aristocrats before the 1950s, upper-class Romans in the period of the Empire found themselves expected to put in periods of service as governors of far-off provinces. In the second decade of the second century, Pliny the Younger was governor of Bithynia (now north-west Turkey). Luckily for the historian, he consulted the emperor, Trajan, at length on matters of difficulty, including the right way to deal with Christians within his jurisdiction.[1] The Christians seemed harmless, but they declined to take part in customary pagan rites, ritual acts of social conformism imbued with numinosity. Not to conform was to be under suspicion of sedition or unreliability. (The reader may think of modern parallels.)

In the course of his description of the Christians, Pliny wrote:

they said that 'they had met regularly before dawn on a fixed day to chant verses alternately among themselves in honour of Christ as if to a god (*Christo quasi deo*)'. As Latin lacks both definite and indefinite article, it is impossible to be wholly sure whether this rendering correctly represents Pliny's sense. If, as is admittedly unlikely, he had taken trouble to understand the Christians' claims or was quoting their talk, then he may be taken as evidence that in less than a century after Jesus' time, Christians in the towns and countryside of Bithynia worshipped him, not as a god, but as God. At the least, Pliny saw them as giving to Jesus the sort of devotion that Pliny saw as appropriate for the gods. Perhaps the chief point is that what was happening was recognizable chiefly as worship (rather than, for example, obedience or philosophical interest). This remains important, however differently from Pliny the Christians themselves would have articulated their claims.

Ignatius of Antioch. At the same period as Pliny was wondering how best to clamp down on Christians in Bithynia, Ignatius, leader of the Christians in Antioch in Syria, was being transported to Rome, where he died a martyr's death. He wrote letters to churches, most of them in Asia Minor (Turkey), in the course of which he refers a number of times to Jesus as 'God' – with unelaborated directness. Jesus is 'God incarnate'. 'Let me imitate the suffering of my God'. 'Our God Jesus Christ.' 'Jesus Christ our God.' These are some of Ignatius' expressions in speaking of Jesus (alongside other terms, such as 'son of God' and God's 'word' which imply, by contrast, distinction between Jesus and God).

Because Ignatius is so bald in these statements, it is impossible to be sure what account he would have given of them. Were they simply dependent on Johannine tradition? Were they largely unreflective, as if to say, 'Never mind explanations, Jesus is God, and that's that'? Or were they assertive over against the claims of others? 'You have your deities, and I have mine – it is Jesus.' In that case they are not unlike Paul's use of 'lord' in one of his statements, 1 Cor. 8.6. But that would mean Ignatius was making no high metaphysical claim, just stating his commitment; and 'deity' rather than 'God' would be the right translation. It would be a limited statement, a comparison. Whatever the precise truth, the root of Ignatius' statements is more likely to be in worship than in careful reasoning. That would come later.

Of course, as we saw in Chapter 3, this language is not in itself unprecedented, even though Ignatius' way of using it, with an attitude, it seems, of 'take it or leave it', is new. It does strike us as a bolt from the blue. The precedents are chiefly in the 'God' statements in the Gospel of John. Whether the background suggested for John's usage in Jewish thinking (p.35f.) carries over into Ignatius is unclear: it looks rather as if the language has become something of a formula ('never mind explanations'): it is something Christians (or at least some Christians) say. The terms expressing distinction-in-relationship between God and Jesus (word, son) had also become traditional (p.34f.). It is the 'God statements' that present us with our problem at its sharpest. How are we to identify and describe the join between Jesus the historical figure, known and observable for a period in Palestine, and Jesus the object of belief – and belief of this extraordinary kind?

AN EXTRAORDINARY BELIEF

There are two sides to the matter. In the first place, the belief about Jesus, in particular the 'God statements', is astonishing, given the Jewish setting in which it arose (despite possible tendencies on some fringes of Judaism, p.36). It is no wonder that Jews have always seen in these claims the great non-negotiable refutation of Christianity's continuity with Judaism. For a monotheistic faith, they seem to constitute a complete break. There can be discussion about precisely which doctrinal statements constitute the impossible offence. The various messianic titles, for example, are cases of mistaken opinion rather than heresy: Jesus and his supporters fall in alongside other messianic claimants of the first and second centuries. The use of 'word' and 'wisdom' imagery for Jesus is more difficult. The strand in Judaism that is represented in the Wisdom literature and Philo did not survive strongly into standard rabbinic Judaism, making its Christian developments in the early period seem at least eccentric. Even to Philo they would have seemed overweeningly ambitious: Moses was the great human presentation of God's word, along with the Law which he mediated to Israel. The Johannine references to Jesus as 'God', if explained in angelic or 'agent' terms (p.36), might be comprehensible, but again so ambitious as to be dangerous. On any showing, the claims for Jesus are surprising and, certainly by the time we reach Ignatius, beyond the pale of Jewish comprehension. That poses the question: How then could such beliefs arise in such Jewish soil? Is it a case of the infiltration of pagan polytheism, flying unseen through the window like penicillin mould into Alexander Fleming's dish? If so, it has proved even more elusive to identify. The imagery and thought-forms of all the early Christian writers are explicable in Jewish terms without remainder – with the single exception before us, so small yet so momentous. Is it a matter of hyperbolic, poetic language? An explosion of uncontainable enthusiasm: 'Jesus is God!'? But the evidence is that, in the culture concerned, that of Palestinian then Hellenistic Judaism, imagery developed along intelligible lines and did not just break out, *anyhow*. Our discussion of various images in Chapters 2 and 3 showed how such development worked. It would be out of character for a single idea, that of divinity, to shoot off at a tangent.

Is it then a matter of sheer revelation? Could this belief about Jesus be a *novum*, truly out of the blue, from God, as it strikes us in Ignatius' use of it? Well, but there is still the matter of the human minds that must be ready and able to receive revelation. As Peter Shaffer's *Royal Hunt of the Sun* showed so poignantly, it was no good expecting the Inca in sixteenth-century Peru to absorb the Thomist-style teaching of Spanish friars: the Inca was not so much resistant or obtuse as just different. There was no way the 'revelation' could penetrate. *This* 'revelation' must have had its point of entry.

So what exactly was happening? Plainly, more was eventually being claimed than 'Jesus is God's agent'. That is probably too low-key a statement for getting the flavour of even the very earliest faith, though it expresses the dictionary sense of many of the terms used. It is certainly a big move from the charismatic figure of historical assessment to 'Jesus our God'.

IDENTIFYING THE PROCESS

We take the development in stages:

1. We saw that faith in Jesus was there from the start. As far back as we can go, that is to Paul and sources that he sometimes uses, Jesus is the object of commitment and not just a historical figure. It is a matter of facts interpreted in the light of belief in Jesus as effective for our well-being in relation to God; or, in more conventional religious language, as 'saviour' and 'lord'. He both conveys God's truth (Mark 13; John 3.12–13) and achieves his purposes (John 17.4–8).

2. As far back as we can go, Jesus was not only the object of commitment and belief, but also the object of veneration and prayer. The belief in him as 'lord', with its backing in Psalm 110.1, easily bore that sense (p.22). The pre-Pauline prayer, quoted by him in Aramaic, 'Our Lord, come' (1 Cor. 16.22), shows Jesus as already one you could pray to. Later in the first century, the Gospel of Matthew, thoroughly Jewish in its culture, stands out in depicting Jesus as the object of veneration, from infancy onwards (13 references in all, notably 2.11; 14.33; 28.17). The word used is not confined to relations with God, but spreads to the attitude proper before rulers; so here it expresses belief in Jesus as messianic king. But whatever the precise connotations in this respect, it is a word of veneration directed towards the figure of whom it is used. 'Worship' is in the picture from the beginning. (See also Rev. 5.9–10, addressed to Christ, alongside 4.11, addressed to God.)

3. In whatever terms people saw 'total commitment', in those terms they had to express it in relation to Jesus. This is a truism: people can only offer what they have to offer, only

speak as they know how to speak. There was no reservoir of accredited statement of belief in Jesus from which to draw. There was one's own understanding of what total commitment would involve, and in terms of that understanding Jesus must be spoken of. The understanding and the speech would therefore differ from group to group, person to person – reflecting the wide range of 'Judaisms' in the first century. But all of them expressed 'total commitment' – that is, within the sphere of those attracted to Jesus. What exactly it was about Jesus that triggered off this response no doubt differed from case to case: his death, his resurrection, his teaching, a particular saying, a particular deed of mercy and restoration. All, in various ways, find their way through into the records that come to us. It is important to see them as distinct routes, not as a comprehensive amalgam, a corpus of belief which everybody must accept. They were more like diverse routes to a destination, which each then sees in the light of the route taken.

4. Somewhere in the fusion of commitment and prayer, sometime in the first century, a crucial line was crossed: Christianity, the 'Jesus group', moved from being a movement in Judaism to being a distinct religion. The earliest symptom of that awareness, still scarcely formed, comes in 1 Cor. 10.32, where Paul speaks of 'the church of God' as a third entity alongside 'Jews' and 'Greeks'. It was to be some time before the import of that categorization came on to the public scene. But the fusion was explosive.

5. Yet this novelty did not come about at the expense of close links with established Judaism. The terms used for Jesus by the first Christians testify to those links. So do the roles in which Jesus is portrayed in the Gospels. However unlike many messianic hopes, he is depicted in messiah-like activities. He is recognizable as, in part, a Jewish teacher or sage. Some Christians put him into the role of Jewish priest (p.39). The newness was far from involving a complete break in religious culture. It would not be all that long before Judaism was to see the rabbi under a comparable range of roles.[2] All the same, there was a change of orientation, from sanctification within the Law to salvation through Jesus. And the change was crucial.[3]

6. That brings us to the second side of the matter, implied on p.60. There were factors in the Judaism of the period which make the move to 'Jesus as God' a little less astonishing than it seems at first sight. These factors have often been disregarded, partly because they were insufficiently realized, partly because the styles of Judaism they represent faded to a large extent, and partly because Christians have been more concerned to establish their distinctiveness from Judaism than to acknowledge their debts to it. The fundamental point is that Jewish monotheism did not at that period involve the utter solitariness of God often assumed by modern theists. We have already shown how many of the terms used for Jesus point to a picture of 'escorts' for God, agents of his purposes in the world. But those terms, mostly broadly messianic in character, do not stand alone.

There was a wide-ranging tendency to view God's mediating of his will by means of concrete, personalized entities of various kinds. There was the personifying of divine attributes, chiefly 'word' and 'wisdom', that was age-old (p.36). They were the vehicle for much Jewish thought on God's cosmic and creative activity. There was the vivid belief in angels, much developed in the later pre-Christian period. They were the vehicle for assisting God to carry out his will and convey his messages to human beings. There were exalted patriarchs from the distant past, like Abraham, Enoch and Moses. They could reveal both the heavenly present and the future course of history until the world's End and after it.

In yet another concentration of images, all three contribute to the picture of Jesus both in the New Testament and later. Jesus was able to step into all these roles in the eyes of those who 'believed in' him. We should even say he *had to* step into them, if those already thinking in such terms were to vocalize their commitment to him. What was new was the identifying of a human being with these roles. To identify him with all three was, again, an explosive mixture.

We have discussed the use made of 'word' and 'wisdom' (p.36). The main exploitation of 'angel' was to come a little later than New Testament times, and it was to be ided by the ambiguity of *aggelos* (Gk): both 'angel' and 'messenger'. As always, scriptural texts imposed themselves. The 'angel of great counsel' in the Greek version of Isaiah 9.6 was identified with Jesus, in the light of the messianic import of the whole passage. On the other hand, Hebrews 1.4–14 shows that writer's concern to counter from Scripture people who see Jesus in angelic terms. It is the first item on the writer's agenda, to show that Jesus was in a class of his own, superior to the angels. As for Jesus in relation to the patriarchs, the story of the transfiguration (Mark 9.2–8) shows Jesus as both like and yet superior to Moses and Elijah (cf. John 3.13: 'no one ascended except'). In Mark 13 he occupies the role of seer that patriarchs or heroes occupied in comparable Jewish apocalyptic books (e.g. Daniel in the Old Testament, and the Books of Enoch).

The effect of these mediating agencies in Judaism was in part to enhance God's transcendence. It populated the heavenly world as densely as the earthly, and linked the two within God's empire or household. Nevertheless, God remained accessible in prayer: the mediators were not felt to block him off. In that way, religion was notably superior to relations to kings and emperors. *God* would hear and act; *they* might or might not.[4]

7. Yet for all that, none of these great agents of God compromised God's uniqueness. In Judaism, none of them quite received worship. Even if Moses had been called 'god to Pharaoh' (Exod. 7.1) and wisdom God's handmaid (Prov. 8.22), there was no question of their receiving divine status. From the perspective of almost all in Judaism, the line was crucial and it was not crossed.[5] From the perspective of Christian devotion to Jesus, it was probably crossed without full awareness of what had been done; like tourists straying inadvertently in open country from one land to another. And as reverence merged into worship, we may identify prayer to Jesus as the instrument which enabled 'Jesus is God' to come into the light. Hurtado calls it a 'mutation in monotheism'.

Putting it another way: the basic Christian sense was, 'God has drawn near in Jesus – no longer does he speak to us from the other side.' Divine transcendence was overcome yet not negated.

As we have seen, Judaism had its ways of asserting comparable belief. Among the Christians it took a small/huge step further: only 'Jesus is God' was adequate to voice the meaning of that step.

The line had been crossed. How to move from commitment and devotion to explanation was the next task. Both among themselves and, perhaps more importantly, in response to Jewish and pagan questions, explanation could not long be delayed. Fundamentally, it was not easy to see how divine transcendence could be both overcome and yet not negated in the person of Jesus. Might new thought-forms, derived from Greek philosophy, prove more amenable to the task than Jewish imaginery and scriptural texts? Might you jettison the latter for the prospects offered by the former and by even headier frameworks of knowledge then available?[6] Might you try to draw benefit from both, philosophy and Scripture, scarcely aware how much at variance they were as idioms of thought?[7] You might indeed do that: for many Christians, both were simply components of the air they had been given to breathe. Partly unawares, Christians found themselves for the first time not just holding beliefs about Jesus but having seriously to conceptualize them. In the next few centuries, problems and solutions cascaded upon them. Old images were adapted or changed out of all recognition, and old ways of believing gave way to new, usually accompanied by strenuous protests of simple faithfulness to the one true teaching about Jesus.

Notes

1   Betty Radice, ed., *The Letters of the Younger Pliny* (Harmondsworth, Penguin, 1963), pp.293–5.
2   Jacob Neusner, *Jews and Christians* (London, SCM Press, 1990), p.14.
3   ibid., especially chs. 1 and 2.
4   This account owes much to Larry W. Hurtado, *One God, One Lord* (London, SCM Press, 1988).

5 The possible exception is the 'location' of God in quasi-angelic figures in some Jewish sources, see p.36. The exact import is unclear and the figures are not human beings.

6 As, notably, in the thought of the numerous Gnostic groups, some of them very influential in the second century.

.7 Some Jewish writers (e.g. Wisdom of Solomon, Philo) had already pioneered such an approach to their own tradition, but it was taken up with much more enthusiasm by the Christian Fathers than by the contemporary rabbinic Judaism.

CHAPTER SIX

Problems and Solutions

DIVINITY COMES FIRST

Modern people usually have no difficulty in seeing Jesus as a human being. Problems arise when it comes to expressing belief in him as divine. We tend to start with the first and work our way, if we can, towards the second. Whether they are believers in Jesus or not, thoughtful people often find it hard to put into words what it could mean for a human being to be 'God'. Often it becomes just an article of faith, to be believed or rejected.

So it comes as a surprise to discover that once Christianity got out into the predominantly Greek world, from the second century onwards, the situation was commonly the precise reverse of ours. Of course Jesus was a heavenly, divine figure who had entered this world; on what terms could he be human? No doubt about the former, considerable difficulty with the latter. It is this underlying contrast in awareness that makes much early Christian belief about Jesus hard for us to grasp. It really does take an effort of sympathy.

Such an effort is all the more necessary because this was the period when classic, normative Christian doctrine was built up. That doctrine remains officially intact to this day, though it is another question how far it is still 'live'. Deliberately or unthinkingly, aspects of it come our way. Whenever Christians go to church, they usually find themselves using its language. Some Christians are 'early Church' when it comes to praying and worshipping, 'modern' when it comes to sitting down to put their faith into acceptable thought. Such situations are not uncommon in the life of long-lasting societies and traditions. Past ideas and customs are not obliterated when new ones arise, but find a niche within fresh settings. There is usually little awareness how out of place, in terms of their origins, these items can be. We are used to the 'wholes' which we see and use, and even applaud their mixed pedigree. Old cathedrals containing elements from every period of their history make a familiar parallel.

So from the second century, in the Greek world, the divine in Jesus had priority. That meant a redistribution of emphasis among the crowd of images and terms which had been applied to him from the earliest days. In one sense, a 'bias towards the heavenly' was already present in all those terms. Even though some of them, notably 'Messiah', had in view a purely human figure, he was nevertheless a figure authorized by God (p.18). As with prophets and priests, equally human, there was a downward thrust, from heaven to earth, implicit in their role. Human they may be, but they were very special humans. But this bias was explicit in other images used for Jesus, notably 'word' and 'wisdom' (p.23). These were heavenly symbols, personified attributes of God, existing eternally. To identify them with Jesus was to claim for him personal pre-existence in heaven. His 'biography' antedated his appearance at Bethlehem.

Seeing him as divine ('Jesus is God') partly stemmed from and partly fortified this imagery. It made a vital bridge from the Jewish world of thought (where it was one line of imagery among several) to the Greek world of thought (where it was wholly congenial and could dominate the scene). Jewish writers like Philo (p.23) had already made use of this possibility, having a foot in both worlds. Christians soon exploited it with enthusiasm. While they continued to use purely Jewish symbols, like Messiah, especially in arguing their case with Jews and establishing a Christian interpretation of messianic scriptural texts (just as the New Testament writers had done), it was the symbols involving pre-existence that soon dominated the building up of thought-patterns. A number of forces pushed matters in this direction. We have only to list them to realize how great an effort of sympathy is now required to enter into the world of the early Christian centuries.

1. Religion as salvation. Partly because of the needs of controversy, both with deviant believers and with outsiders, the Christian thought of this period was often (as it seems to us) excessively theoretical, worrying over points of nice abstraction and of little practical importance. But if getting the theory right seemed vital to the Christian thinkers of the period, it was usually because they were dealing with issues which to them were essential for religious effectiveness. They were articulating a religion before they were elaborating a theology, and their overriding concern was with *salvation*. In their eyes, that was what a faith existed to provide. Therefore a saviour from outside, capable of freedom from the constraints and disabilities of earth-bound humanity, was essential if the remedy were to succeed. What was the good of a doctor who was himself infected by the diseased situation which he must put right?

This is clearer if we realize how the human need of salvation was seen. We get a flavour of it already in 1 Cor. 15. 42–55: mortality and corruption (i.e. being subject to rotting and dissolution at death) are the two great enemies that Paul there identifies. The great Christian thinkers of the succeeding period echo and intensify that feeling. Salvation must involve some way of deliverance from these two horrifying, negative aspects of the human lot. They form the framework for – and are the penalty for – moral alienation from God through sin.

In such a climate, it is no wonder that one of the earliest disputes among Christians was between those who insisted that 'Jesus Christ has come in the flesh' (1 John 4.2) and their fellow-Christians who saw that as of no use at all: for the latter, the rescuer must be immune, wholly from outside. So widespread was this sense that we can almost characterize those whom we look back on as the 'orthodox' Christians as those who managed, in an adverse cultural situation, to maintain a belief in the humanness of Jesus and to see point in it. Often, as we shall see, they scarcely did it to our modern satisfaction; and often it was at some cost to the coherence of the intellectual presentation of their faith. Putting it another way, they were those who maintained the closest hold on the Gospel picture of Jesus and on the Jewish heritage, where physicality had more positive value.

The contrast between then and now is vividly seen in relation to the gospel stories of the virginal conception of Jesus. For modern people who wish to take them as historically or doctrinally significant the problem is likely to be with the non-human element. Of course Jesus had a human mother – no problem. But how to make sense of the absence of a human father? For the early Church of the Graeco-Roman world, the problem was precisely the contrary. Why exactly should the divine one involve himself *at all* with the procedures of human conception? And the orthodox assertion, keen to maintain his humanness, was: Well, he did have a human mother, and isn't that as much as (indeed more than) one could ask? It was a gesture of infinitely generous divine condescension on his part to enter so far into our human situation and human ways. The idea that the condescension might have been more impressive if there had also been a human father would have been a tasteless complaint. The lord of the manor came to our house: who are we even to entertain the thought that he might also have shared our food? Moreover, such a complaint flew in the face of the increasingly literal interpretation of the birth stories, including the interpretation of the term 'son of God', now seen as focusing on Jesus' divine paternity (p.21).

2. Platonist perceptions. The feelings of religious need and propriety just described melded perfectly with the dominant Platonist outlook of the period, which had itself developed strong religious overtones. It centred on a sense of the absolute contrast between God and all else, the divine and the creaturely, the 'real' world of ideas, perceptible only to the mind, and the world of phenomena, open to the senses. Once again, this differs sharply from our way of thinking, whereby reality is to be found primarily in what the senses perceive, then secondarily, if at all, elsewhere. The absolute contrast extends to the attributes found on the two sides. Change and decay, visibility and describability on the one side; eternity, stability, invisibility, ineffability on the other. As we have seen, this sense of the divine as utterly 'other' in relation to the human was closely connected with its role as effective saviour. All the same, it made a faith which spoke of a divine one in human form hard to put into concepts. How could any figure unite two such incompatible entities with their contrasting properties? Such a thing was either impossible and incredible, or else it was a great and mighty wonder, beyond all expectation. At precisely this point, pagan and Christian thinkers divided.

3. The chain of being. One way of mitigating the difficulty, which chimed in with a widespread way of thinking, was to place Jesus on the scale of beings which populated the universe. Nowadays we tend to arrange the world in our minds in terms of species, substances, and categories, with their various sorts of interrelationships. It scarcely occurs to us any more to think in terms of a unified hierarchy of objects, in which the spiritual element becomes more and more rarefied the further down we move and the physical element more and more crude or dense. Sometimes, we still rank animals in this way: lions are said to be the rulers of the animal kingdom, though we know it is a fantasy. But supposing that the universe really is arranged, below God, in a chain of angels, humans, animals, reptiles, fish, plants, and inanimate objects, where might Jesus fit? There are overlaps of characteristics on the chain: angels and humans can both worship their creator knowingly; humans and animals both have similar digestive and reproductive arrangements; plants lie around immobile like inanimate objects. So if we place Jesus at the top, just above the angels, or perhaps in a class of his own, might it not be possible to see him sharing characteristics with us, such as thought and speech, and the closest relationship with God, the fount of all life and all things? In some ways, this picture, while doing justice to Jesus' heavenly 'base', cut across the Platonist picture, and in due course, decisions had to be made about which of the two did more justice to Christian faith. Meantime, the chain of being had its uses, and it had links with parts of the Jewish inheritance, with its belief in angels and its symbols of divine agents like God's word and wisdom. As we saw in Chapter 5, some Christians saw Jesus in terms of a super-angel. It was an idea that, as a formal belief, soon faded from theological discussion, though it retained a toe-hold in liturgy, perhaps down to recent times. The picture of a hierarchy, in which Jesus had his place, continued to play a part for some time longer. Some Christians (Gnostics), soon labelled as dissident, placed Jesus in and among all kinds of hierarchies, and in the second century the diversity was chaotic.

This collaboration of religious impulse and philosophical ideas was effective in bringing the divinity of Jesus to the fore. It entailed, however, the playing down of certain aspects of the story of Jesus. Where they accorded ill with assumptions about the divinity, they were presented in ways that strike us as evasive or artificial. Sometimes they were simply dropped. Thus statements in the Gospels about Jesus' hunger (Matt. 4.2) and ignorance (Mark 13.32), indicating human weakness, were explained as instances of the divine one graciously and fittingly accommodating himself to human conditions: in other words, gestures rather than parts of normal human life, humanly experienced. Like an adult deliberately adopting a child's perspective for the sake of a conversation or a game, it was a matter of an outsider generously identifying with an alien situation, making it his own for the overwhelming good of salvation. Sometimes the fact that the world, fallen as it was, was God's creation, was held on to only with some difficulty.

From the standpoint we are describing, the suffering and death of Jesus were more difficult to interpret than any other aspects of his story, crucial though they were known to be. Here above all there seemed to be exposure to change and weakness. Yet how could this be true of the divine of whom immunity to suffering (impassibility) was a necessary characteristic? One solution was to hold that the suffering did not really 'get to' that inner divinity. The place of its attack was the human body, which was indeed Jesus' 'own', but was the instrument through which the inner 'he' acted on the human scene. A passage from the fourth-century Alexandrian bishop and theologian, Athanasius, illustrates this cast of mind:

> The priesthood of Aaron under the Law prefigured that of the Messiah. Now, as Aaron was a man before he was a priest, and his priestly vestments did not change his nature, but only his outward appearance . . . in the same way, there is no reason to suspect that any alteration befell [Christ's]

eternal nature when he assumed ours; but what we are to
understand . . . is only that he united our nature personally
to his. It is impossible to fancy that the eternal Word of
God, as such, should in process of time 'become' or 'be
made' anything whatsoever which he was not before. But
that, as being the creator of all things, he should make or
create himself a body, when the fulness of time was come;
that he should make himself our high priest; that he should
join this body to his divinity, and then offer it up to atone
for our sins; this is intelligible enough.

(*Orations against the Arians*, II.8.)

In a historical perspective, matters sometimes went even
further. Eusebius, bishop of Caesarea, published his innovating
work, the *Ecclesiastical History*, in the 320s, shortly after the end
of persecution and the heaven-sent favouring of the Church by
the emperor Constantine. For Christians, it was a time of triumph
and euphoria. Eusebius takes his story back to the beginning –
but to our eyes it is a strange picture of the beginning. Though
the death of Jesus is alluded to, it is always *en passant*, and it
is never described or discussed, unlike other episodes in Jesus'
story. Eusebius tells a tale of success, and it is as if Jesus' death
had no easy place in such a context. We are a long way from
the proportions to which the New Testament writers worked.

The early part of Eusebius' *History* illustrates another
consequence of the perspective of 'divinity first' in this period.
We have seen that from the start Jesus' person and career were
interpreted by Christians by way of Old Testament texts. The
Old Testament as a whole was regarded as prophetic, whatever
the kind of literature involved (legal, historical, hymnic, etc.).
The belief in the pre-existence of Jesus led to a further dimension of Christian understanding of the Jewish Scriptures and
a further means for their incorporation into the Christians'
heritage. We saw how that belief came into the range of
Christian understanding of Jesus through the application to him
of the Jewish images of 'wisdom' and 'word' (p.37). Because
of its prominence in the opening of the Gospel of John and
because the term had useful connotations of mediatorship in

the prevailing Platonism and Stoicism, 'word' soon came to predominate. In much Christian discussion (see, for example, the extract from Athanasius above), Jesus was seen as 'the Word' (= *Logos*, Gk). As such, he had been active from 'the beginning' – in the creation of the world (John 1.3), in the thought of the great pagan philosophers (so believed some Christians from the second century), and in the Old Testament. From being the one to whom those Scriptures pointed, he became also a prominent actor within the story they told. The Gospel of John already made this inference: it was not the transcendent God himself whom Isaiah saw in the temple (Isa. 6.1–8), but Jesus (John 12.41); and he existed before Abraham himself (8.58). From these beginnings, the method blossomed luxuriantly. It was the Logos (not the transcendent Father) who walked with Adam in Eden and appeared to patriarchs, and who spoke to prophets and heroes. The Old Testament was a Christian book, in that it was a book about Jesus. Eusebius begins his history by giving some of the classic instances; but he had many predecessors, and by his time the argument was well established. Both eternally (from 'the beginning', before the creation) and throughout history, the divine Logos, identified with Jesus, had existed and acted. In the reading of the old Scriptures, the 'bias to the heavenly' in the picture of Jesus was constantly before Christian eyes and received its most practical application.

An interesting corollary, once more a surprise to most modern perception of the subject, was that from one angle the total novelty of the incarnation was diluted. The Logos became 'flesh', and that was momentous – a new dispensation had dawned – but from another point of view it was simply the addition of a dimension to a long-known presence. A permanent actor in the drama adopted a crucial new costume. It was no wonder that so much attention focused on the precise understanding of that human costume, and that the long-standing personalness of the Logos' involvement in the world made it hard to see the plain human Jesus in rounded, self-contained human terms.

PROBLEMS OF THEORY

Religious impulses and religious needs were at the root of the modes of belief about Jesus that came to the fore among Christians once the Church moved out of its Jewish setting into the Graeco–Roman world. Those impulses were no longer quite the same as those of the first years, and religious needs, though always centring on 'salvation', came to be perceived with what we have called a bias to the heavenly. Belief which already in the early second century expressed itself in terms of 'Jesus our God' dominated the scene.

Such belief secreted in itself intractable problems of intelligibility. They would be raised by outsiders, both Jews and pagans; and they would be raised about insiders who looked as if they were stating Christian belief in one-sided or erroneous forms. Two major questions were inevitable:

1. How can Jesus be seen as God without making nonsense of the claim to monotheism? However forcefully Christians pressed their assertion that Jesus fulfilled the Jewish Scriptures, and however strong their arguments, using the methods of the time, that Jesus was the clue to the Scriptures' 'true' meaning, it was hard to rebut the assertion that those Scriptures were plainly about the one and only God of the universe. What was more, Christians did not wish to be taken as saying that they believed in two Gods. They hotly refuted polytheistic pagans who claimed them for their side of the fence, just as they refuted the pagan charge that their religion was merely a bastardized form of Judaism, unworthy of respect.

Until the fourth century, most mainstream Christians worked with some form of the belief that Jesus (and, in so far as this came into the discussion, the Spirit) was secondarily divine. He had his place as derivative from God but above the angels in the scale of being (p.72). 'Second God', used of Jesus by Justin in the mid-second century, was not wholly outrageous even in Jewish terms, being applied occasionally to mediators such as we described in Chapter 5. And though Jewish Scripture was monotheistic, there were texts which could be read as implying pluralism within the divine sphere (as indeed Jews could read them in terms of the various mediators): witness, for example, the 'us' in 'Let us make man in our own image' (Gen. 1.26) and the mysterious trio of heavenly/divine visitors to Abraham (Gen. 18). Much, if not everything, hinged on the meaning to be given to 'the divine sphere'.

It was when the question of the bounds of that sphere was pressed in the early fourth century, in the dispute surrounding Arius, that the demands of the Platonist picture (God versus all else) came to predominate over the claims of the 'chain of being' picture (p.71f.). Then there had to be a decision: on which side of the vital frontier did Jesus stand? The issue was forced, and no longer could he be seen as, however loftily, vaguely straddling the frontier, or taking his high place in a stream of ever less concentrated deity.

The question may or may not seem unreal to modern people, depending perhaps on how far we succeed in immersing ourselves in the issues at stake. We should be clear that it was not a question of deciding whether Jesus was divine or a mere man: few Christians saw the matter in those terms, and scarcely any believed the latter. He was the pre-existent Logos, living in heaven from 'the beginning'. The question was how exactly the character and location of his being, 'derived' from God (the Father), were to be expressed. It is true that some Christians, when using the Logos terminology, seemed to think in terms of an attribute of God (his word or thought) which only at the incarnation, becoming linked to the human Jesus, reached personal status. But they were rarely consistent in that view and rarely confined themselves to it. It was a picture that yielded to the more 'full-blooded' idea of the personal Logos/Jesus.

There were teasing intellectual problems here, but it is a mistake to think that that was all there was to it. Once more, religious sensibilities were at stake. We may get a feel for them if we substitute royalty for divinity, and put ourselves in the shoes of royalty-admiring people. How far do we see royalty as a quality diffused through a range of persons (the royal family) or does it truly belong only to the monarch? Though the monarch is undoubtedly the head and fount or royalty, to what extent and in what respects does it reside specially in that head? Might that headship itself be shared? Then, does royalty become less intense or concentrated the further down the line of 'royals' we go? Or is it a quality which, if possessed, is absolute, regardless of where the person stands on the family ladder? A consideration of these questions, as much ones of feeling as of plain thought, illuminates much of what was at stake in the early Christian centuries, as Christians themselves, largely for their own internal purposes, had to work out more exactly what they believed (and needed to believe) about Jesus.

To swing the matter still further in the direction of feeling and to get a sense of what was at stake religiously, try putting yourself in the position of royalty-admiring people who wish to attract royalty to some function which enlists their loyalty. Will there be equal pleasure whether the monarch or instead a mere secondary or tertiary 'royal' agrees to grace the day? Or will it make all the difference whether the monarch comes in person; and if the monarch will not come, would the whole project lose all steam? Might the heir to the throne do (almost) as well?

Must the Logos be firmly on the divine side of the frontier to be effective for salvation – which is our vital interest? Or will it suffice for him to be more vaguely 'heavenly' or 'divine'? In the fourth century, Christians came more and more to see the place of Jesus in terms of those questions. Did he, or did he not, need to be 'fully' divine, for salvation, which he had brought, to be effective and intelligible?

2. The second major issue concerned the conceptualizing of the divine in Jesus in relation to the human. We have already seen that in this period the weight most commonly fell on the divine side. The personal pre-existent Logos was, as it were, 'fully formed' in heaven. The incarnation was (whatever the language of John 1.14) more of an adding than a becoming. But what exactly was added? If it was only a human body, which might seem all that was needed for him to be perceptible in the world, then was not Jesus human in a seriously defective way? Was this not a pseudo-humanity, and the whole exercise irretrievably bogus? Whether it was seen so would depend on

how great an importance was given to 'full humanity' in this case.

We have already seen that philosophical ideas and religious feeling conspired to produce a low demand in that direction. For many Christians, the immune doctor was the model; and even for those who felt more of a need for the Logos' genuine identification with the human condition, it was not usually at the expense of wonder at the condescension which had brought the divine one to visit and redeem his people. The fairy-story image of the prince incognito among the peasants was rarely eradicated totally, and few had any compelling wish to exclude it. The democratizing of Jesus was not a major pressure until much more recent times. Modern Christians, singing Charles Wesley's 'Hark! the herald Angels sing' at Christmas, do not perhaps realize how limited a view of Jesus' humanity is expressed in the line 'Veiled in *flesh* the Godhead see'. By most fourth-century standards it is impeccable.

It would be anachronistic to credit Luke with the perceptions of a later period, and certainly wrong to accuse him of mischievous foresight, but what problems he caused for his Christian successors when he wrote of Jesus growing in wisdom (2.52). How could the divine Logos *grow* in any respect whatsoever, beyond the merely physical? And supposing his humanness really was more than 'flesh' and included 'mind', would that not impair the Logos' directive role in Jesus? Would it not introduce a competitor? And if the competitor was present but never competed, was it not a mere automaton? Yet its presence was surely essential if a sense of Jesus' real humanity, a sense of the Jesus of the Gospels, were to be insisted on, and if his effectiveness to save human beings were to be really credible. In fact, this, rather than historical or psychological realism was the primary consideration.

The Christian belief in Jesus – now in himself rather than as relating to divinity – was faced with cruel dilemmas along these lines in the fourth and fifth centuries. Tunnel-visioned, rival religious demands (*either* his being divine is all that really matters for our salvation *or* genuine humanity also matters) were not easily brought to negotiation. Such settlement as was achieved (at Chalcedon in AD 451) was more successful at the verbal level than in terms of religious understanding, or strict logic, or even permanent ecclesiastical political arrangement. Once the belief in Jesus in terms of the personal pre-existent Logos had taken almost universal hold, it was virtually impossible to hold it together with a realistic belief in Jesus' humanity, whatever forms of words were attempted. Either the Logos needed no such 'fully human' companion or instrument, or there was no easily imaginable basis for the union of the two. Tandem riders and those whose calling it is to inhabit in pairs the skins of horses in pantomimes can appreciate the problem. That it was pitched at a theoretical rather than such a practical level in our period does not altogether remove the helpfulness of the images.

The first of the two great questions, concerning the divinity of Jesus, bequeathed to the Church the Nicene Creed (AD 325 and 381), still recited in the liturgy of the great Churches: Jesus Christ is 'God from God . . . of one substance with the Father'. The second question bequeathed the less known Chalcedonian Definition (AD 451): Jesus must be seen in terms of two natures (divine and human) in one person. The formulas conceal not only much protracted controversy but also conflicting religious instincts, or different ways of picturing the place of Jesus in relation to the human need of God. There is always a measure of achievement when those at variance agree on a form of words. But interpretations of words differ and deeply valued patterns of believing are not obliterated.

Beliefs about Jesus mattered too much and were too closely linked with everyday religious practice to be greatly affected by decisions of councils, however august the imperial auspices under which they met. They were, for example, intimately bound up with eucharistic belief and practice. To eat the eucharistic bread was to share the divinized body of Jesus, and so oneself to be transformed. In this context, it was essential that the 'flesh' should be the flesh of the Logos: or where would be the salvific value? For most Christians the miracle of redemption was that the Logos came at all – and then remained available in the sacrament. Words were found, even in circles where the idea was not felt as pressing, to show that the Logos did indeed unite full humanity to himself; but the effective initiative remained with the Logos, for in him lay the only route to salvation. The need to safeguard that unique route was so great that it was surrounded by a sacred enclosure: it was in this period that devotion to Mary began, with her new title 'Mother of God' or 'God-bearer' (or, for others, seeking more balance of the human side, 'Christ-bearer').

The modern Christian who is accustomed to use some of the words and formulas of this period may slip into some of its attitudes and concerns with relative ease and indeed find them deeply moving. It will be surprising if these attitudes have the monopoly of thought and prayer. It will be equally surprising if the words are understood quite as they were first coined. To turn from them, in our modern way, to the Jesus of history is to be made to gasp. It is hard to deny that, along with all the technical theological language and devotional feeling of the period, the triumphalist Jesus of Eusebius' perception held sway. Jesus was king of kings, the emperor's emperor. Political religion, a new phenomenon for Christians, chimed in harmoniously with the existing bias to the heavenly. But it entailed a muzzling of Jesus' revolutionary impact, his transforming and challenging of human hopes and confidence. For Eusebius and his contemporaries it was clear that Jesus had manifested God, and that was what mattered. It is when we consider what they thought he had manifested about God, his character and his moral priorities, that we may have cause to object.

CHAPTER SEVEN

The Pattern Modified

A FIXED PATTERN?

It is not difficult to point out logical flaws and untidy elements in the pattern of beliefs about Jesus whose emergence was described in the last chapter. In the Church as a whole, there were different emphases in belief, and these did not disappear just because bishops had gathered and pronounced at a council. In institutional terms, the chief among the different emphases were embodied in Churches that became separate and, from the point of view of the main body, marginal: Monophysites, holding to the utter predominance of the divine in Jesus, and Nestorians, holding to a sort of parity of humanity and divinity in Christ. In the turbulent politico-doctrinal history of Eastern Christendom, these elements have persisted in various forms down to the present day.

Despite its flaws and the refusal of some to accept it, the pattern was established. It too has persisted to the present day. It may have been hammered out by bishops in books and councils, but it has permeated all levels of Christian life, by way of creeds and hymns, catechisms and prayers. The flaws were countered, the structure made more watertight. From long use and by means of rational argument, it came to seem unassailable. It became part of the fabric of all the main Christian Churches, and Christianity was unimaginable without it. So indeed it remains, in the official teaching of all those Churches. In Eastern Orthodoxy and in large tracts of Catholicism, it remains unchallenged. But in Western Christianity, especially in parts of the Churches of the Reformation, it has been subject to overt challenge for three hundred years and, as we can now see, to erosion for a great deal longer.

'Erosion' is a term that hindsight brings to mind. From a point of view within the process of development itself, the matter looks different. At the level of formulation, the pattern which was worked out in the centuries after New Testament times, remained firm and solid. It became the classic, sufficiently watertight scheme of Christian belief. At the level of perception, devotion and practical belief, there were however crucial changes, which had their own validity and made their own kinds of sense. The patristic pattern of the early centuries, worked out in dispute and debate, was amazingly durable, but not as durable as those looking at the matter in official or theoretical terms often suggest. Words may survive; what people 'feel' the words mean is rarely static. This chapter relates to the most influential of the changes which took place. It brings us closer in thought as well as in time to our own situation, though we should beware of acknowledging kinship too quickly.

THE DIVINE HUMANITY

The period from the later eleventh and twelfth centuries saw a shift in sentiment and values which is variously described as 'the discovery of the individual', 'medieval humanism' and 'the troubadour spirit'. Asked to locate Sweetheart Abbey, many people would guess that it was an eccentric religious foundation (or perhaps a hotel) in California in the 1960s. In fact it was a Cistercian abbey established in the 1270s near Dumfries in Scotland, by Dervorguilla, in memory of her beloved husband, John Balliol.[1] Life within monasteries, especially those of the Cistercian Order, had from the time of their rapid expansion in the early twelfth century been marked by a new candour of mutual affection. Relationships were expressed in passionate language, and the modern reader is often puzzled to find little evidence that this extravagance of word was matched by physical act and did not always signify even personal acquaintance with the one addressed. (For example, in some of the letters of Anselm of Canterbury in the second half of the eleventh century.[2])

Belief about Jesus in the classic pattern centred on his awesome power and his cosmic rule. He was the Creator–Logos, who in the period of his earthly visitation had done great miracles, finally vanquishing death and dispelling the ills of our mortality. The man of Nazareth was but the screen for the Logos, and to have met Jesus and to have touched even the hem of his garment was to have encountered the Creator of all things, now made visible. This style of belief accorded well with the Church's 'arrival' as the religion of the Roman Empire in the course of the fourth century, and Christ the super-emperor presided over the social and political hierarchy, in imagination and art as well as in theology.

The death of Jesus itself was seen less in terms of suffering and horror than in terms of triumph and victory. Such a view appears in the New Testament, in Paul (Col. 2.15) and in the passion narrative of the Gospel of John. But in the context of the classic pattern of doctrine it had its head. In words, carvings and pictures, Jesus was depicted on the cross in crown and royal robes, head erect, reigning over the universe. The cross itself was viewed as a kind of throne, the vehicle of a royal triumph; as in the sixth-century hymn of Venantius Fortunatus:

> The royal banners forward go;
> The cross shines forth in mystic glow . . .
> O tree of beauty, tree of light!
> O tree with royal purple dight!
> Elect on whose triumphal breast
> Those holy limbs should find their rest.

To move to the hymn, *Jesu, dulcis memoria,* dating from about 1200, is to find oneself in another world.

> Jesu! – the very thought is sweet!
> In that dear name all heart-joys meet;
> But sweeter than the honey far
> The glimpses of his presence are.
>
> No word is sung more sweet than this:
> No name is heard more full of bliss:
> No thought brings sweeter comfort nigh,
> Than Jesus, Son of God most high . . .
>
> Jesu, thou sweetness, pure and blest,
> Truth's fountain, light of souls distrest,
> Surpassing all that heart requires,
> Exceeding all that soul desires!

No tongue of mortal can express,
No letters write its blessedness:
Alone who hath thee in his heart
Knows, love of Jesus! what thou art.

The adjective 'sweet' (Latin, *dulcis*) is a watchword of this style of devotion. Close to it is new emphasis on the heart, as the seat of emotion and of religious strength, somewhat displacing the will and the mind. The name of Jesus as an instrument of power (for healings and exorcisms) has Semitic and biblical roots (e.g. Acts 2.38; 4.30), and its constant repetition in prayer goes back in Eastern monasticism at least to the sixth century. Now it is more overtly the object of fervent love. Its use *forms* the soul, evoking the feeling of universal and personal loving care. True, the hymn quoted above contains a verse referring to Jesus in older terms as 'wonderful king' and 'noble victor', but it goes on immediately to address him as 'ineffable sweetness, wholly desirable one'. It is clear where the stress now lies.

In the same period as the hymn, or somewhat before it (the earliest example is from the 970s), crucifixes began to be what we see as 'realistic' depictions of the event of Jesus' execution. The head is bent, eyes closed, body stripped, wounds visible, blood flowing. But we should take care. This realism is not historically but devotionally and doctrinally motivated. It is not a case of 'we must depict Jesus' death as it really was'. The mode is still iconic; only the icon has changed: from 'Jesus our prince' to 'Jesus our loving saviour'.

In the following centuries, Jesus who loves us, whom we in return must love and whom in his dying we must pity, comes more and more before us. The conventional motif, in painting or sculpture, of the pietà, Mary nursing and lamenting the dead body of Jesus, dates from the thirteenth century. Its verbal companion comes in the hymn, *Stabat mater dolorosa* ('At the cross her station keeping/ Stood the mournful mother weeping/ Close to Jesus at the last'). It is no surprise that the image of Mary and the infant Jesus underwent change comparable to that of the crucifix. Earlier, the child had sat as if enthroned in his mother's lap, holding symbols of power (an orb) or of wisdom (a book). Now the solemn figures staring out at their faithful subjects give place to more relaxed and natural attitudes. Once more, however, it is not the naturalness of history that is involved, but the naturalness of the relationship of devotion. It is typified in the spread of the Christmas crib, whose invention is credited to Francis of Assisi in the early thirteenth century. The new Franciscan Order was prominent in the popularizing of this more humane way of believing in Jesus and of believing about him.

The change we have been describing was no temporary phenomenon. It was the beginning of a process which has continued, comprehensibly if often surprisingly, to the present day. That is partly why works of the period remain popular and accessible: the hymns, the paintings, the sculptures, and the writings. None illustrates this ethos better than the work of the fourteenth-century mystic, Julian of Norwich. For example:

> After this, Christ showed me the part of his passion near his death. I saw his sweet face as it was then, dry and bloodless, with the pallor of a dying man: deathly pale with anguish . . . The showing of Christ's pains filled me full of pain. For though I knew well that he had suffered just the once; yet he wished to show me his pain and fill me with mind of it, as I had before desired of him. In all this time of Christ's presence, I felt no pain except for Christ's pain . . . and like a wretch I repented me.
>
> (*The Revelations of Divine Love*, chs.16, 17)

Her work includes the most vivid descriptions of every stage, every smallest aspect of Christ's suffering. Yet again, however, the interest is not historical realism or exactitude, not a concern to 'get the story right'; it is devotional and theological realism, a concern to identify with full fidelity with Jesus' act for our salvation.

The same judgement applies to a later stage of development. It was already common, indeed from early Christian times, to interpret the Song of Songs in the Old Testament as an allegory of Christ's relationship with the human soul. In the poetry of John of the Cross in the sixteenth century this theme receives erotic treatment:[3]

Let us rejoice, Beloved [= Christ],
And let us go to see ourselves in thy beauty
To the mount or to the fell
Where springs the clear water . . .
The breathing of the air,
The song of the sweet nightingale,
The grove and its gentleness
In the peaceful night,
With a flame which consumes but gives no pain.

Finally, before we try to pinpoint the significance for our purpose of this style of belief, we note a manifestation of it which, perhaps more than any other, forces us to recognize that this is not a humanistic or personal view of Jesus of a modern kind. In the period of the Renaissance, from the fourteenth century onwards, hundreds of depictions of Jesus as nude appeared, in paintings, sculptures and altarpieces. Many of them are in Mary and child compositions, but many are representations of the crucifixion or of the deposition from the cross. Though 'natural' in the sense that the figures are straightforwardly human, they are doctrinally representational in intent. Here God the Father, arrayed in crown and royal robe, aged and bearded, supports the corpse of Jesus, the former placing his hand over the latter's genitals. Sometimes Mary is shown making the same gesture. Such a depiction would now be unlikely to pass the scrutiny of those who select works of art for churches, and if it did the public outcry is not difficult to imagine. Are we right to see ribaldry, and even to suspect blasphemy? Or is it that, while we would be bound to see such a work as 'historically', purely naturally representational, its context was quite different for those of the fifteenth and sixteenth centuries? What would that context have been?[4]

We have already seen enough evidence to suggest that we should look in the direction of devotional-cum-doctrinal sensibilities. It is not a matter of formal and official beliefs about Jesus having changed; but it is a matter of those beliefs being 'felt' in new ways; and sometimes, as we shall see, there were new theories to match the feeling.

It is necessary briefly to retrace our steps. In the early Christian period, when the classic pattern of belief was being established, two distinct emphases emerged: on Jesus as dominantly divine, and on Jesus as the focus of union between divine and human. The latter emphasis 'solidified' by the fifth century as Nestorianism, but it had long had representatives in both Western and Eastern parts of Christianity. Among those who shared this approach, with their sense of the importance of Jesus' *complete* humanity if his saving role were to be effective, the practice arose of dividing up Jesus' words and actions in the Gospels between the two sides of his person: it was as God that he stilled the storm and fed the multitude, as man that he felt hunger and grew in wisdom. Each of his two natures was in effect a bundle of attributes and characteristics which could be seen as coming into play at different stages of the life and death of the one, single Christ. It is natural now to feel an artificiality about this picture. It is not easy to relate to one who seems to operate like a machine powered now by one battery, now by another. It was possible to find forms of words to express his unity of person, harder to find a realistic way of seeing it.

Or so it came to seem. In the medieval period, a new approach to Jesus' humanity presented itself, that which was responsible for the developments which we have described. What was now felt vividly was the paradox and appeal of the divinely-human one, a truly human being and the 'seed' and source of restored humanity, one with us to the most minute particular, with whom we could identify most intimately, yet divinely so – therefore sinless and exemplary. This was the doctrine illustrated in the nude and even sexual presentations of Jesus. Doctrine, probably in this case that of the 'wholeness' of Jesus' humanity, meant that he was depicted as uncircumcised, despite Luke 2.21. History still gave way before the doctrinal pattern, however realistically it was presented. It is no wonder that this way of believing often centred on the crib and above all on the passion, in all its realistic detail and sheer pitifulness; no wonder that it occasioned much weeping and laughter, sorrow and joy; no wonder that love spilled over into extreme mortification and penitence. This is the period when detailed meditations on Gospel episodes were elaborated and propagated. It was a mode of devotion that was at home in the monasteries and spread to the literate laity – and further, through stained-glass windows, statues and book illuminations. It affected all levels of church life.

Those who might be thought special guardians of pure formal doctrine in the period, such as teachers in the universities, could express themselves with total correctness by traditional standards, yet the new note was also present: in one of his hymns written for the new (thirteenth-century) feast of Corpus Christi, in honour of Jesus' physical presence in the sacrament of the Eucharist, Thomas Aquinas wrote: 'On the cross only the divinity lay hid, but here (i.e. in the sacrament) the humanity is equally concealed. But believing and acknowledging both, I in my penitence seek what the thief sought.' The allusion, to the story of the crucified thief, who asked Jesus to receive him into Paradise (Luke 23.43), brings the formal doctrinal statement immediately into the sphere of the personal, and it is no accident that the reference is to the most personal and 'human' of the Gospels. It is a Jesus who is wholly accessible. The detailed *imitation* of Christ becomes a major Christian goal.

The same fusion of orthodox doctrine and vivid, emotive realism can be seen in the carving high in the arch of the north porch of the cathedral at Chartres which depicts God's creation of Adam. If it were not in a sequence showing the story of creation and fall, it would be taken for Jesus healing a young man or perhaps raising from death the son of the widow of Nain. In terms of traditional doctrine ('through him all things were made', John 1.3, via the Nicene Creed), the carving is impeccable: it was the Logos who created Adam – that was the standard interpretation of the story in Genesis 2 read through early Christian eyes. The thirteenth-century sculptor has no quarrel with it; but this is no formal, abstract Logos, no actor in a conceptual scheme of formal doctrine, nor even a figure in the Christian myth. It is the personal Jesus here at work, evoking in the observer a personal, warm response of love. We identify with Adam, the object of creative care, who owes all to the figure standing above him, giving him life.

In at least one way, this sensibility was matched at the level of theoretical speculation, and it is not surprising that it was developed in Franciscan academic circles, notably by Duns Scotus, in the thirteenth century. It was religious exuberance about the human that led to the belief that though the incarnation had in fact occured as a rescue act, a remedy for sin, it would have happened anyway – God simply delighting to unite humanity to himself.

Devotion to Jesus as our mother seems at first sight to fall into a different category from the instances we have been noticing. Found in Anselm and notably in Julian of Norwich, the idea of Jesus as mother looks simply like an image for loving care and self-sacrifice, especially appropriate in relation to the passion. But if we enter more closely into this devotion, we discover that it is close in character to the language of Jesus as lover, and the one is neither more nor less direct than the other. Both are rooted not so much in what we should recognize as sheer emotion or sentiment as in basic Christian doctrine: once more, devotion and doctrine are intertwined. Julian wrote: 'For in our Mother Christ, we have profit and increase; and in mercy he re-formeth and restoreth us.' 'I saw and understood that the high might of the Trinity is our Father, and the deep wisdom of the Trinity is our Mother' (*The Revelations of Divine Love*, ch. 58). Jesus is mother as our comprehensive life-provider, in both creation and restoration, through his incarnation.[5]

JESUS IN THE SOUL

The dialogue between Jesus and the soul, modelled on the imagery of the Song of Songs, which John of the Cross (and many others) portrayed, was also doctrinally impeccable in traditional terms, but the ethos of this writing, now so prominent, was very different from that of earlier times. Jesus the king had become Jesus the lover. But in writing of that kind there was a further implication, one whose effects were in due course to be far more revolutionary – this time in terms of doctrine.

Works like the poems of John of the Cross were in effect

imaginary dialogues, conducted interiorly, between Jesus and oneself. This was prayer in the form of conversation. To concentrate on that interiority was to move right away from reference to Jesus as a historical figure (or, for that matter, as the subject of abstract doctrinal formulas). It related to an intensely felt personal present; not to the past, nor to the realm of timeless truth. It is no long step from religious awareness of this kind, concerned with Jesus in the soul, to a more or less frank abandonment of history.

In the England of the Civil War and its aftermath, in the middle of the seventeenth century, censorship of publications was temporarily removed, and people could express their genuine thoughts. In such circumstances, underlying tendencies of belief come frankly to the surface. Many radicals like Gerrard Winstanley and William Erbery distinguished sharply between the human, historical Jesus and Jesus in the Christian soul. The Wiltshire Ranter, Thomas Webb, said: 'We did look for great matters from one crucified at Jerusalem 1600 years ago; but that does us no good; it must be a Christ formed in us'.[6] Such statements were not made in the interests of historical investigation into Jesus' life, still less in an anti-religious spirit. Their concern was spiritual, with Jesus as the inspirer and companion of the Christian. From a realistic historical viewpoint, it still involved an idealized Jesus and perhaps an inherently docetic Jesus – one whose humanness was less than central to the attention, indeed candidly pushed aside. Already it was a version of that division between the Jesus of history and the Christ of faith which became so prominent in more recent times.

Such pushing aside of the history was a crucial step. Ultimately it made it possible to take the further step of examining the history of Jesus for its own sake, on 'neutral' terms. If faith could (or even should) subsist independently of the history, then the history could be examined independently of faith. The ground was prepared for the historical study and the historical hypothesizing about Jesus which have marked the past two centuries and more. Not until history became autonomous could that investigation escape the constraints (as they came to be felt) of dogma and the susceptibilities of devotion. It was now possible, in principle, for reverence and faith to be set aside; and in time, aprioristic reasonings, whereby 'correct' answers and attitudes were prescribed in advance of investigation, came to seem artificial and unacceptable. Or so they came to seem to some: to many they seemed, and seem, nothing of the sort. As we have found before, the Christian tradition keeps going somewhere within itself every element to which it has ever given birth.

Thus on the Catholic side, old unities survived, with the sacred humanity of Jesus still exerting its power. Devotion to the Sacred Heart of Jesus, formalized and popularized from the eighteenth century (though somewhat demoted recently), and to the Sacred Heart of Mary and the Precious Blood of Jesus (heyday in the nineteenth and earlier twentieth centuries), kept alive and vibrant the style of believing about Jesus which this chapter has described. The Pietist tradition, prominent in Lutheranism from the seventeenth century, then among Moravians and Methodists, preserved the same impulse on the Protestant side and has ensured its continued vitality. The music of J. S. Bach, above all the Passions of St Matthew and St John, is perhaps its greatest monument. They were composed in the Age of Reason!

Notes

1 See R. W. Southern, in *Oxford Today* (February 1991).
2 R. W. Southern, *Saint Anselm* (Cambridge University Press, 1991), pp.138–65.
3 E. W. Trueman Dicken, *The Crucible of Love* (London, Darton, Longman & Todd, 1963).
4 See Leo Steinberg, *The Sexuality of Christ in Renaissance Art and Modern Oblivion* (London, Faber and Faber, 1984).
5 See Grace Jantzen, *Julian of Norwich* (London, SPCK, 1987), pp.115–24; and C. W. Bynum, *Jesus as Mother* (University of California Press, 1982).
6 Christopher Hill, 'Irreligion in the "Puritan" Revolution', in J. F. McGregor and B. Reay, eds, *Radical Religion in the English Revolution* (Oxford University Press, 1984).

CHAPTER EIGHT

The Pattern Challenged

THE AUTONOMY OF KNOWLEDGE

The independence of history as an object of investigation was the most far-reaching ingredient in the revolution in belief about Jesus that began to take place in the early modern period. This attitude to the past was reached by a number of routes, of which the last chapter identified one. More broadly, advances in knowledge meant that some people could no longer see biblical history as other than myopic. Great empires – Assyrian, Babylonian, Roman – could no longer be viewed merely in terms of their biblical and church role. What the Bible said about them and their role in church history were partial perspectives. Those sources supplied some evidence, but not all of it, and their contribution was often grossly one-sided. Biblical characters, including (implicitly at first) Jesus himself, began to shrink into life-size actors on a large stage.

To take a wider view, autonomous history was one of a number of parallel developments in the sixteenth and seventeenth centuries, which erupted piecemeal but had shared characteristics. The astronomical discoveries of Copernicus, Kepler and Galileo undermined biblical data such as the notorious backward-moving sun of Joshua 10.12–13. Geographical discoveries subverted mental (and actual) maps of the world which centred on the Mediterranean or even Jerusalem. Distant and strange races made the story of Adam's creation look parochial and discoveries about ancient civilizations made the biblical dating difficult. Palliatives like I. de la Peyrère's hypothesis of the race of pre-Adamites (1655) were hugely popular.

Closer to our subject, the stabilization of Western Europe as partly Protestant and partly Catholic meant that by the mid-seventeenth century the long hegemony of a single religious authority was over. In the structure of the situation, though not at all in practice for most people, choice was available: it was possible, even necessary, to look again at the evidence. For some, that meant re-examining Scripture with new candour. Chiefly in Poland, from the mid-sixteenth century, Socinians anticipated the commonplaces of modern biblical interpretation by taking Scripture on its own terms and without presupposing the apparatus of official doctrine. The chief casualty was the doctrine of the Trinity, and so of Jesus' divinity; in effect, the classic pattern of belief about Jesus, as the incarnation of the Second Person of the Trinity. So, now by another route, the human Jesus again stepped to the fore. Here, the Reformation's own principle of basing belief on Scripture alone began to lead to the subversion of the classic beliefs which the central teaching of the Reformation had continued to maintain.[1]

Whether it was a matter of the scriptural piety of the Socinians or the secular proposals of the astronomers, geographers and historians, the autonomy of thought and discovery was plain to see. Implicitly, and soon explicitly, this meant the assertion of human reason as a principle superior to the authoritative utterances of Churches, whether in past or present. The ground of reason and knowledge was one on which pope and student might (they never do!) meet on equal terms. For many, Scripture remained the source of religious truth; but they too brought external criteria of truth rather than sheer authority or tradition to its interpretation. By so doing they in effect helped to bring the intellectual battle onto the territory of reasonable argument. Belief about Jesus is henceforward part of this scene.

In the case of belief about Jesus, however, there was a twofold movement. The figure of Jesus played a part in two increasingly distinct spheres: that of historical study and that of the theoretical study of Christian theology. Reason was appealed to in both areas, but it was reason in what emerged as two different senses or applications. There was reason as applied to concepts, theories, ideas; and there was reason as applied to evidence of a factual kind – documents, events, archaeological remains. The two overlapped in some respects in relation to Jesus. Some matters integral to belief about him had a foot in both camps, notably those that involved the miraculous: the resurrection, the virgin birth, and many other elements of the Gospel story and of the creeds. So belief about Jesus was bound to figure in both kinds of enquiry. To begin with, those involved in the subject often investigated in both areas, and in both the historical and the philosophical spirit. But as time went on, they became more and more distinct. Philosophers and theologians on the one hand, historians and biblical scholars on the other, drew apart. Today they often write without much heed of each other's conclusions. What is commonplace and obvious from one angle is unobserved from another, and Jesus figures in debates of extraordinary variety.

With regard to Jesus, the autonomy of knowledge and enquiry meant the autonomy of the human. A particular writer might hold more or less orthodox beliefs or wholly secularized beliefs about Jesus, but the treatment of the subject came to proceed more and more as if the human Jesus could alone be the basis for discussion – whatever else might then be claimed about him. Whether the miraculous was seen in terms of proofs of divinity or as against reason, instances were examined in historical terms. The more biblical scholarship extended its imagination into the subject of Jesus, naturally the human Jesus dominated the scene. The mind was dedicated to the capturing and evoking of the human past. By the mid-nineteenth century this was already so vividly done that people could feel a closer and more 'accurate' affinity with Jesus as a first-century Palestinian figure, very distant in time and (for most) in space, than could (let us say) Origen writing less than two centuries after Jesus' time and near to Jesus' own land, but with his mind fixed on him as the eternal divine Word who, briefly, visited his people. The two perspectives and projects of belief are worlds apart. It is of course another question how far those who in recent times imagine themselves into the setting of Jesus, even with the full panoply of available knowledge, deceive themselves. It is, however, clear what is being attempted and claimed: a making 'real' of the human Jesus.

Equally, the emphasis on evidence and on event and fact influenced the sphere of concepts and theories, just as, reciprocally, developments in philosophical ideas gave confidence to those working in the sphere of history. Theories of reality which put the weight on the senses and on observation necessarily diverted attention away from ancient patterns which depended on a 'bias to the heavenly'. The classic scheme of belief about Jesus came to seem unrealistic, over-explicit in its picture of the divine, over-precise in its language of substance and natures.[2] Sometimes, the reaction was a frank rejection of the whole Christian scheme of things; but sometimes it was as if the challenge to the pattern gave even to believers a kind of licence to see belief about Jesus in new ways, to express it in terms of fresh leading ideas, which, by comparison with the old, spoke only vaguely of the 'other world', even if fully confident of its power and reality. In this way, 'reason' manifested itself not only in negative, harsh dismissal of belief in favour of sober historical assessment, but also in terms of multitudinous new forms of belief which, with varying adequacy, took account of historical realism.

And of course there were stops at all stations between the two, and (to alter the metaphor) surprising attempts to run with the hare while hunting with the hounds. In effect, whether you wished to jettison the faith which the traditional pattern of belief had embodied or to retain its 'essence' while seeing it in a new light, reason had put the pattern into the melting-pot. No longer could the pattern be taken for granted. Increasingly, it seemed inadequate, either wholly or in certain aspects, to express what seemed credible about Jesus.[3] Even among those keen to retain it, it has been the subject of extensive modification, sometimes 'sold' as re-expression.[4] In what follows, we shall see examples of all these tendencies at work.

The autonomy of knowledge and of the human, with roots far back in medieval times but maturing in the seventeenth and eighteenth centuries, gave rise to twin progeny whose legacy remains: rationalism on the one hand and romanticism on the other; the purifying and isolating of reason as a tool in investigation and the purifying and developing of imagination as a faculty of mind and spirit. Of course the two are at variance: to the latter, the former seems static in its perception of reality, over-confident about a particular style of thought and cramping to the spirit; to the former, the latter seems undisciplined in thought, too much exposed to human vagaries, too credulous. When it comes to Jesus, both styles have been at work, at both scholarly and popular levels: Jesus the subject of abstract argument (how could he be divine and human? how could he rise from the dead?) and Jesus the focus of imaginative warmth (what was Jesus really like? even, especially in the nineteenth century, what must it have felt like to be Jesus?). These two kinds of sensibility (they are wider than philosophies or theories) have dominated both theological debate and religious life for at least two centuries. Official, orthodox belief continued (and continues) to have many defenders, some subtle and skilled, others more conservationist in spirit; but from both the reason-led and the imagination-led points of view, belief in the personally pre-existent Jesus of classical doctrine faded, and where it survived, it took more arguing for; and the old sense of personal, quasi-biographical continuity between the eternal one and the historical figure was eroded. Whereas in earlier days, above all in the patristic period, the weight fell on the pre-existent dimension, now it fell more and more on the Jesus of the historical manifestation.

More recent perspectives, from the legacy of Marx (Jesus as a figure in the socio-historical process) and of Freud (Jesus as subject to psychological development) have only served to reinforce this tendency. Everything conspired to create and to express a less formally dogmatic and a more personal apprehension of the divine, whether manifested in nature or in the human spirit – or in Jesus. J. H. Newman wrote on the fly-leaf of his copy of his own book, *Essay on the Development of Christian Doctrine*, 'Revelation is not of words'.

FACT, CONCEPT AND FAITH

Almost every feature of subsequent debate is to be found, at least in embryo, in seventeenth- and eighteenth-century Western Christianity. Despite many different phases and turns of debate and of fashion, the major ingredients were all present; from one point of view, they were implicit in Christianity from the very start (p.12). The three chief ones were: fact – Christianity involved past events in principle open to scrutiny; concept – the events must be interpreted in the light of rational ideas and criteria of truth as currently perceived; and faith – attention to the events and their elucidation is fuelled by commitment to the figure of Jesus in the context of belief in God. During the past two centuries, the ingredients have been mixed in varying proportions, but for almost all who have expressed themselves on the subject of Jesus, all three have played some part. The story of belief during the period is to a large degree the story of the relationship between them: their rises and falls, their interplay, and their frequent disregard for the claims and potentialities of one another.

FACT, AND THE PRIMACY OF EVENTS

At the scholarly level, investigation of the life of Jesus and its setting has had the lion's share of attention. All this work has had remarkably little effect on popular beliefs about Jesus, partly because the subject has lost its former centrality. Nevertheless, it bears some responsibility for the general feeling that old beliefs, such as the resurrection and the virgin birth, are historically questionable. In church life, it has never managed to find a way of conveying widely either its methods or its results. The rocks of traditional creeds and liturgies have so far found it impossible to treat a realistic historical approach to Jesus as other than swirling, threatening waters. A handful of modern hymns[5] convey something of its ethos, and sometimes realization of it causes bafflement. It seems hard to assimilate.

In its own context, however, historical study of Jesus has given rise to many different beliefs about him. From the time of Reimarus in the mid-eighteenth century, and indeed in even earlier English writers, one strand, found in many guises, has deconstructed the Gospel story to such an extent that traditional doctrine has been wholly subverted. Suspicion has focused on the stories of the passion and resurrection. Suppose they represent a cover-up, with the truth being what the Gospel of Matthew already found it necessary to refute: the disciples stole the body of Jesus and put about the story of his rising from the dead to boost the fading fortunes of their movement. Jesus himself was a moral teacher and messianic pretender who came to Jerusalem, trusting to elicit the divine intervention on which his mission hung, or perhaps to die as a martyr in God's cause. As much political as religious, he died in failure, the victim of Roman suppression at least as much as Jewish opposition. Or perhaps he did not die at all, but merely swooned into unconsciousness, only to be temporarily rescued and revived. The variants are numerous. The effect of such conjectures on belief has a single tendency: to make traditional doctrine sustainable only by extreme effort and to make even the human Jesus all too fallible, at best a tragic figure meriting pity but scarcely eliciting faith.

However, it has been possible to share much of this picture and yet invest the Jesus it presented with major religious significance. The leading example of an ability to find faith-eliciting nobility, even in Jesus the disappointed preacher of God's great future for the world, was Albert Schweitzer who, at the beginning of this century, in *The Quest of the Historical Jesus*, presented the story of the nineteenth-century attempts to delineate the Jesus of history. For him, Jesus, the mysterious apocalyptic preacher, certainly spoke of 'the Other' and drew religious commitment, but his aim was to direct our religious self to realities beyond himself and beyond definition. Jesus 'does not require of men today that they should be able to grasp either in speech or in thought Who he is . . . The one thing he does require of them is that they should actively and passively prove themselves men who have been compelled by him to rise from being as the world to being other than the world, and thereby partakers of his peace.' 'He commands. And to those who obey him, whether they be wise or simple, he will reveal himself in the toils, the conflicts, the sufferings which they shall pass through in his fellowship, and, as an ineffable mystery, they shall learn in their own experience who he is.'

So this strand of belief, focusing on Jesus as the messianic preacher of the kingdom of God, could encompass debunkers and almost mystical adherents. It included both elements of historical good sense and, in the hands of some writers, implausible reconstructions motivated more by modern ideologies than a sound sense of historical probabilities. There are cases of strange bedfellows. Both modern Christian liberationists, and people understandably stung into reaction by the long Christian tradition of assigning all blame for Jesus' death to the Jews, have seized on Jesus as the holy Jewish freedom fighter whom the Romans could not tolerate.

Another strand, prevalent particularly in the nineteenth century, also involved a highly selective and deconstructive approach to the Gospels. It highlighted aspects of Jesus congenial to the times, such as his high moral teaching. The Sermon on the Mount now leapt to the fore as a ground on which all decent persons could agree in admiring Jesus, even if they found traditional doctrines about him difficult. Sometimes to the consternation of ethicists, only recently has it become apparent that the so-called Sermon in Matthew 5–7 is part and parcel of the theological outlook of the Gospel of Matthew as a whole.

To highlight the ethics was to demote not only the theological but also the miraculous, which, under the pressure of 'reason' as well as by historical judgement, was credited to the constructive religious imagination of the early Church. Miracle stories, now to be seen as legendary, were the natural way for first-century Christians to express their devotion to Jesus and their dawning religious convictions about him. They were dispensable from the standpoint of Jesus' permanent religious significance. D. F. Strauss' *Life of Jesus* (1835) brought this approach sensationally into public view.

A romantic strand sometimes allied itself to the moral, even slipping over into the sentimental. Ernest Renan's *Life of Jesus* (1863) achieved vast popularity. Marginalizing the miraculous, he did not in the least lack enthusiasm for his version of Jesus the man, 'a glorious human countenance full of life and movement'. Schweitzer, whose own picture was so much a reaction against both the moral and the romantic approaches, was scathing: 'The gentle Jesus, the beautiful Mary, the fair Galilaeans who formed the retinue of the "amiable carpenter", might have been taken over in a body from the shop-window of an ecclesiastical art emporium in the Place St. Sulpice.'

All these strands presupposed the 'autonomy of knowledge'

and the autonomy of the human to which it gave rise. Behind and alongside them lay the steady process of 'neutral' historical study of Jesus and his context. This study was not of itself concerned with the formation of 'beliefs', and even consciously eschewed any such role. Lessing's dictum, from the mid-eighteenth century, is squarely behind the great tradition of historical enquiry, best represented in the following period by F. C. Baur of Tübingen: 'Accidental truths of history can never become the proof of necessary truths of reason.' Formally neutral with regard to traditional beliefs and indeed all religious beliefs about Jesus, such study was likely to give the impression that history left religion with much hard work to do. Jesus was a Galilean prophet about whom his followers came to believe remarkable things. 'The nature and the reality of the resurrection lies outside the sphere of historical enquiry', wrote F. C. Baur (1853). 'What history requires as the necessary antecedent of all that is to follow is not so much the fact of the resurrection of Jesus, as the belief that it was a fact.'

We have already seen that not dissimilar understandings of the history can be either compatible with belief in Jesus (however expressed) or with no religious beliefs about him (p.56). In the relationship of historical enquiry and faith, it is possible to point to instances of every position on the scale: from those whose pre-formed faith about Jesus determines their reading of the historical evidence to those whose historical scrupulosity compels them to eliminate faith as unreasonable. Certainly the more Jesus is seen in the confines of his historical setting the more difficult it is to make claims for his significance for all persons, of all times and places. Where faith is asserted, it comes to seem more of a preference, an arbitrary attachment of meaning to *this* significant figure of the past among so many, than a claim (e.g. to divinity) which commands attention and carries inherent authority. All this remains applicable to the developments of recent times, in the work of such scholars as Martin Hengel and E. P. Sanders, making ever fuller and clearer the realities of the Jewish setting of Jesus' life. If Jesus is seen in an even broader biblical perspective, that of the religious history of Israel, there may be a valuable spin-off for Jewish–Christian understanding, but, with his career seeming but an important episode in that history, wherein can his cruciality lie and how can it be presented? Faith may still assert itself, but some diminishing of stature (a taking seriously at last of the human in Jesus?) seems inevitable.

CONCEPT, AND THE PRIMACY OF IDEAS

There have been many in the modern period for whom concern for the historical evidence about Jesus has not been primary. Some of them have expressed beliefs about him in largely abstract terms; others have attended to the history, in particular to the Gospels, but the driving force, the imaginative pressure, has come from concepts rather than the detailed literary and historical evidence itself. Sometimes, only a hair's breadth, hard to discern, separates them from those chiefly attached to historical enquiry, but to their companions firmly in that camp they often seem insufficiently critical of the evidence and over-determined to substantiate a picture that is conceptually formed.

On the more abstract side, we point to a strand in which the empirical, human Jesus plays a subordinate and even a detached role. He is the instantiation of an idea or principle which is greater than he. If he is the object of faith, then that is the role in which he functions. What really matters, however, is our mental perception of the archetype of moral life, pleasing to God. Jesus stands as our model of that archetype and so our encourager. What is involved here is not a critical evaluation of the Gospel record, but a general appreciation of Jesus' character. So Immanuel Kant in the later years of the eighteenth century. Or else, for Hegel in the following generation, Jesus is the historical instance of eternally valid spiritual realities. For Paul Tillich, he embodies and mediates the 'new being'. Or else, for Teilhard de Chardin in the middle of the present century, Jesus is the 'omega point', the goal of consummation, already manifested in history, to which the whole cosmic evolutionary process tends. In this strand, the actual characteristics of Jesus the historical figure virtually disappear.

Another strand has focused more on the human Jesus in his

own right: as the vantage point from which we can look to God. Again, Jesus is the exemplar, but now much more crucially, not just the convenient illustration of truths already and otherwise known. Friedrich Schleiermacher's perception of Jesus is a natural development, in his early nineteenth-century setting, of the old German Lutheran and Moravian pietistic tradition, itself in continuity with late medieval devotion to the human Jesus, Jesus within the believer's soul. To shed the formal, traditional language and conceptual patterns of classic Christian belief was not a massive move for that tradition. But now it led to a way of believing that began firmly from the human and observable Jesus, with whom the believer is identified. In his *Life of Jesus*, based on lectures given in 1832, Jesus is the one who moved towards the perfection of awareness of God and of relationship with him. Here the history was real, but nevertheless subordinate to the idea – of 'God-consciousness' – and to faith. There was little difficulty in uniting this perspective with what might be called a soft doctrine of incarnation: 'To ascribe to Christ an absolutely powerful consciousness of God and to attribute to him an existence of God in him are entirely one and the same thing.' Interestingly, emphasis on the 'consciousness' of Jesus as the heart of his mission enabled Schleiermacher to set light to the miraculous element: in this case, 'reason' by no means banished faith, which stood in no need of miracles.

Though modern in his sense of Jesus as a Jew of his time, the tendency of Schleiermacher's doctrine was not without precedent. In the third century, Paul of Samosata had taught that Jesus was the greatest prophet of all, in whom God's 'word' was present in the highest degree – different from others, therefore, in degree and not in kind. In the prevailing ethos ('bias to the heavenly'), Paul of Samosata's name became virtually synonymous with heresy of deepest hue. Schleiermacher met the same charge from upholders of the tradition; and so have his successors who have tried to review the classic pattern in the light of modernity along his lines, in effect seeing divinity in Jesus as the supreme instance of God's grace as found in the rest of us (see notably D. M. Baillie's famous *God was in Christ* [London, Faber and Faber, 1948]).

If this strand represents an attenuation of the traditional pattern from a standpoint that is strong in faith, others have candidly put Jesus in the light of a colder framework of ideas. Historical investigation of itself leads to no plain conclusion about Jesus as a focus of the miraculous; it can simply describe the evidence. From the early nineteenth century and before, there were those who read the Gospel stories as tales, based on observation but told by the simple and the credulous. In reality, Jesus the edifying teacher had no such impossible powers. The stilling of the storm stemmed from the coinciding of Jesus' word and a natural calm; the feeding of the crowd from Jesus' blessing of a host of packed lunches. The imposition of such rationalizing, found both in Germany and among some twentieth-century English modernists, shows little understanding of the evangelists' own framework of belief, but it touches on a matter which had other manifestations. If Jesus were truly human, and further belief about him must work from that basis, then, supposing such further belief to be attempted, how might divine attributes be understood? Omnipotence (which might indeed still storms and feed multitudes) vies with the limitedness inherent in being human. So does omniscience; so does impassibility.

So-called *kenotic* (from the Greek for 'make empty', used in Phil. 2.7) Christology is best known from the work of Charles Gore, especially in *Lux Mundi* (1889). It sought to retain much of the classic pattern of belief but to combine it with a perception of Jesus' human life that was both rationally and historically realistic. Thus, at the incarnation, the pre-existent Word did not, as in the traditional pattern, merely abstain from using the full range of his divine powers, but truly, if temporarily, put them aside; so that Jesus on earth knew only what was appropriate for a person of his time and place to know, and truly suffered as (indeed more than) any human would. The idea has seemed to lack realism: what kind of identity is there when one phase of existence blots out all consciousness of another? It seems difficult to retain the idea of Jesus' pre-existence at such a price. In effect, there is a confusing of two worlds of thought: one derived from early Christian Platonist patterns, the other from modern historical and rational realism. Such disparate partners now seem incompatible.

However, of all the traditional attributes of God, and so of his embodiment in Jesus, the one that has occasioned most difficulty is his impassibility. We have seen that attention to the stark reality of the suffering of Jesus has been central in Christian devotion since medieval times. The same has naturally been true of those looking at Jesus more recently in a historical spirit: of course he suffered as any human would suffer. More, any exemption, at any level of his being, would invalidate his capacity to be 'one of us', 'the man for others'. Especially in the latter part of this century, with its plethora of human disasters and the media-made worldwide awareness of them, it has come to seem not only that belief about Jesus must find a way of accommodating the utter, unequivocal reality of Jesus' suffering but that it must see that genuine suffering as the centre of his manifestation of the divine. For some, it has been necessary to go further still. It is in his suffering that Jesus supremely reflects God, for God is a suffering God. So Jürgen Moltmann in *The Crucified God* (London, SCM Press, 1974), a book that struck resonant chords in many minds.

So strong has been the pressure in this matter that even some avowed defenders of the traditional pattern have felt impelled to adjust it to accommodate divine passibility. It seems not always to have been recognized that adjustment at this point is, however, no piece of minor tinkering or repair. From the broad historical point of view adopted in this book, the idea of God's *im*passibility was at the very heart of the traditional pattern, and we saw that from the start there was implicit tension, at this point especially, between the pattern and the data of Jesus' life and death as depicted in the New Testament. However ingenious the attempts at accommodation between the pattern and the new compelling insight on this subject, does not the abandoning of belief in Jesus' impassibility-as-divine really entail the subversion of the pattern as a whole? However admirable philosophically modern improvements to the pattern may be, why saddle oneself with 'the problem of Jesus' in *that* form in the first place? Again, ideas from such contrasting worlds can scarcely be held together without strain. What would make the strain worth enduring?

With greater candour and boldness, there is a strand which asserts the misguidedness of attempts to press belief about Jesus, if it is to be genuine religious and theological belief, into moulds formed by external criteria of truth and of reason. Such attempts are doomed. Intellectually, their effect is to forbid God to act as faith perceives him to have acted in the person of Jesus (and indeed in the whole process of revelation). In this sense, the primacy of reason meets its head-on critique. It is a rejection not in the name of history, nor in the name of arbitrary faith, but in the name of a mode of reasoning which subordinates itself to the God-given data – chiefly to his disclosure of himself for human salvation in Jesus. Here the overwhelming divine initiative in Jesus, which lies at the heart of the classic pattern, has been preserved, without the loss of a realistic sense that the subject is the human figure of the Gospels. For Kierkegaard in the early nineteenth century, the sheer unexpectedness of belief in Jesus as the junction of divine and human, the sheer unprovability of the claims of faith, were their greatest testimonies. For Karl Barth in the present century, God's word, manifested in weakness in Jesus, has precedence over human attempts to make sense, whether rationally or historically. For Rudolf Bultmann, his contemporary, there is indeed profound respect for historical enquiry and he made the greatest of contributions to the historical study of Christian origins, but his picture of Jesus is as the one from God who, within his historical setting, simply summons us to decision, for or against the cause of God: as an existentialist before his time. In this way, the history, which may indeed embody strong elements of accuracy, is the vehicle of the idea; and reason is both used and countered. Indeed, Bultmann draws the sharpest line between the history of Jesus, with its uncertainties, and his God-given saving role, on which the 'facts' have no bearing: for faith, he is simply the revealer who summons us to accept his call.

Dietrich Bonhoeffer's famous characterization of Jesus as 'the man for others', which John Robinson popularized in *Honest to God* (London, SCM Press, 1963), seemed to speak of an attractively human Jesus, free from the clutter of dogma and abstract concepts. The strength of his sense of the secularity of the modern world and of the need for the gospel to find 'non-religious' ways of entry into such a world did indeed introduce a note of stark realism. 'What is bothering me incessantly is the question . . . who Christ really is, for us today', he wrote in prison in 1944 for his part in the bomb-plot against Hitler, a year before his execution. But his lineage was that of impeccable German Protestantism and his chief debt theologically was to Karl Barth, and he is not to be read as 'selling out' to a picture of some humanistically ideal Jesus who causes no difficulty to secular people.

The legacy of the prominence of reason in the eighteenth century was many-sided and complex, its interplay with history rich and diverse, the degree and nature of its openness to faith and its determination by faith varied and subtle. Over most of the period, few removed themselves from a world of thought which saw the issue of belief about Jesus as central for religion. Few were unaffected by the independent but related claims of history and of reason, even in the act of rejecting them.

FAITH

This third element has already made numerous appearances in relation to the roles of history and reason. In relation to the latter, it has made its purest contribution where argument to back faith has been renounced, as in the case of Kierkegaard, and even more where the possibility of divine 'backing' has been disclaimed altogether. There have been atheists who have 'opted' to believe in Jesus – whether as moral example or as spiritual inspiration or as fount of a tradition which can now survive on the strength of the figure of Jesus even if all metaphysical doctrine has lost its power to convince. On this strange, but possibly prophetic fringe, writers like Don Cupitt and Alistair Kee have placed themselves. Where belief in God has disappeared, belief in Jesus may occupy the floor all to itself.

It will have become apparent that the strands which have just been identified are only distinguishable with some difficulty.

Perhaps it was only worth attempting the task in order to present the matter of beliefs about Jesus in the past two centuries in an assimilable manner. Likewise, there are often good reasons for placing some of the individuals referred to in categories different from those in which they appear here. It seemed better to include imperfect examples rather than no examples at all. But in a scene of such riotous diversity, itself a result of the 'space' created by the sapping of the traditional pattern of belief on an unprecedented scale, leading writers and thinkers have often represented different aspects of available sensibility, even while thrusting chiefly in one particular direction. Immersed in the scene, they were not always in a position to stand back and ensure their own coolness and consistency in representing a single well-defined position. Most of them have been Christian believers, associated with church life, a factor that has added a dimension to, and provided a context for, their use of history and adoption of intellectual perspectives in such a way as sometimes to confuse rather than to clarify.

Indeed, the period has been marked by a series of much publicized 'rows', each representing one or another strand in the challenge to the traditional pattern of belief, and each greeted as if unprecedented and outrageous in the novelty of its proposals. Yet each has simply drawn upon perceptions which it had come to seem impossible to deny, and impossible to assimilate to the full-blown traditional pattern or perhaps to any version of it whatsoever. In Great Britain alone, we may trace the periodic explosions on the subject of belief about Jesus from that occasioned by Gore for his contribution to *Lux Mundi* (1889), to that surrounding H. Hensley Henson's appointment to the bishopric of Hereford in 1918, and on to the publication of J. A. T. Robinson's *Honest to God*, and of *The Myth of God Incarnate* (London, SCM Press, 1977). In addition, there is the well-known difficulty experienced by William Temple (subsequently Archbishop of Canterbury) over the 'miracles' of the virgin birth and the resurrection as he approached ordination at the beginning of the century, and the uproar surrounding the earlier period of David Jenkins' episcopate at Durham. The list is not exhaustive. With variations, in all cases the issues have been much the same: the attempt to see a way to maintain the centrality of Jesus while taking due account of a range of awareness deriving from history or from reason in some form or other. In each case, some interference (at least) with the traditional vocabulary and so with the pattern of thought it expressed was involved. The irony has been that few of those outraged have been able to give an authentic or convincing account of the full classic pattern of belief to which they ostensibly held – so many and such varied aspects of modern consciousness and modern education cried out against it in its full rigour. To many, however, to tamper with it overtly has seemed inadmissible.

Yet the very fact of the outraged feelings says something significant about modern belief about Jesus. How is it that the subject is still one that can occasion such feeling, such anxiety, such love? On what basis can debate now proceed and what are the prospects for the future?

Notes

1 For the foregoing, see Klaus Scholder, *The Birth of Modern Critical Theology* (London, SCM Press, 1990).
2 'Substance', to refer to the one divine 'being' shared by Father, Son and Spirit in classic Trinitarian doctrine; 'natures', to refer to the two sets of attributes or centres of reality, one divine, the other human, to be found in the single 'person' of Christ.
3 Some of the most brutal 'exposures' of the difficulties of the classic pattern in a cool, modern light are to be found in the poems of Stevie Smith, especially 'Was He Married?' and 'Oh Christianity, Christianity', *The Collected Poems of Stevie Smith* (London, Allen Lane, 1975), pp.389, 416. But the figure of Jesus still fascinates and intrigues her; see 'The Airy Christ', p.345.
4 Not surprisingly there are also ironies and confusions. Sometimes modernity and tradition find themselves allied. Thus feminist sentiment, saddled with the undeniable maleness of the Jesus of history can take advantage of the traditional pattern to bring out what its authors never quite envisaged in support of such a cause, that is the 'genderlessness' of the Godhead, and so of the pre-existent Christ. They can also claim, with the classic pattern's

support, that in the incarnation it was human nature not maleness which was *essentially* assumed by the divine. Those opposed to the feminist cause, notably with regard to the ordination of women, find difficulty in circumventing at this crucial point the traditional doctrinal pattern to which they are also normally attached.

5 e.g. Patrick Appleford's, 'Lord Jesus Christ, you have come to us,/ you are one with us,/Mary's Son'.

CHAPTER NINE

Debates and Prospects

THE LEGACY OF HISTORY

It is a contradictory culture in which the past is both despised
for the sake of modernity and valued for the sake of 'heritage'; in
which knowledge of the past is less widespread because education
must include so much else, and yet every brick of old buildings
must be preserved intact. In such a culture, Churches, heirs to
a vast yet specific tradition, are in a peculiar position. They
feel a solemn responsibility to their tradition, such as few
other institutions can even rival (colleges? regiments?); yet
their members share the wider culture, with its frequent
ignorance of the past and its strange determination to hold
on to it at all costs. Often, the greater the ignorance, the
cruder the determination. Yet the past that is preserved is, in
part because of the ignorance, a sloganized past. It consists of
isolated fragments of the past that, for modern reasons, come
before the eyes (some piece of Scripture or item of formal belief).
Mostly, it is also a decontextualized past. There is little sense of
a total setting (for Scripture, for ways of stating belief); and so,
for many, little sense of how different the past was from the
present, and of what one might be taking on board in using
its words and appealing to its authority.

All the same, the Churches are the only place we have where
the Christian past can be preserved in such a way as to take it
seriously as a usable, even a life-giving tradition, telling us of
God. Others, in the world of scholarship, will preserve it as a
body of knowledge, often with greater candour about it than
can be depended on in the community of faith. In the matter
of Jesus, concerning both the history surrounding him and the
long history of belief about him, both Church and scholarship
have their own concerns and their own responsibilities. That
Jesus should be a subject of intense interest in both spheres

but in quite different (though variously overlapping) ways is the result of the process that we have been considering.

What is undeniable is that the weight of belief about Jesus, in both past and present, rests heavily on both kinds of shoulders. The subject is inescapable, at least for anyone wishing seriously to inhabit Western culture in any of its many ramifications. It is also, as we have seen, infinitely complex, chameleon-like. Whenever we try to pin it down, exceptions will be cited, disagreements and misunderstandings pointed out.

But first, and most fundamentally, there is the sheer dominance of the figure of Jesus in the history of Western culture: in painting, sculpture and music; in great institutions such as monasteries and universities; in political theory; in the steady habits of everyday life of prayer and Eucharist; in the punctuating of life at baptism, marriage and death; in the omnipresent symbol of the crucifix; in the inner conviction of him as personal saviour for countless thousands, from the apostle Paul to the latest convert. Even to talk of present decline or ignorance is partial and local: there are England and France, but there are also Ireland and Poland. There is the widespread churchgoing of the United States, the massive and lively spread of Christian belief in Africa and South America, whether in traditional or wholly novel forms. There is the central role of Christians in the revolutions in Eastern Europe in 1989. In that sense, and regardless of one's own beliefs, the figure of Jesus is undeniably well and truly alive.

Yet, if we survey again the same vast expanse of past and of present, there is the utterly bewildering variety of images of Jesus. People have believed in and about him in ways that may indeed be seen as related, as thought and sensibility evolve from one period to another, and we have traced some of these relationships; yet it is inadequate to view them simply as a series of similar items, like a sequence of shots of the same person or scene in an album of photographs. In the first place, some of the images are contradictory: Jesus the freedom-fighter and Jesus the super-emperor; Jesus the overthrower of authority and Jesus its legitimator; Jesus the friend of the poor and powerless and Jesus the endorser of the powerful and established; Jesus the lover and

Jesus the moralizing judge; Jesus the Jew and Jesus the figure in a Hellenic philosophical scheme or cultic pattern; Jesus the European (in effect) and Jesus the African or Asian; Jesus the puritan and Jesus the libertarian; Jesus the warrior and Jesus the man of sorrows. In the second place, we cannot simply juxtapose the images and make no attempt to assess them – whether because of the contradictions just noted or because of the time-bound character of some of them. We must ask whether validity of a kind is conferred on images just because they exist or have been influential and helpful; or whether some images are just mistaken, even travesties of 'truth'. Further, how far should the beginning of the history ('Jesus as he really was') dictate boundaries to belief about him?

There is a riposte to the catalogue of diverse images which says that they reflect the proper universality of Jesus. But the question has to be raised whether one who is universal in the way that has been described really stands for anything. Does he not become simply a figure who adds nobility and sublimity to any and every human ideal and aspiration? Sometimes indeed (the Nazi Jesus) he adds only a sententious cackle of solemnity and endorses wickedness. He seems to be available to add divine validation to what people see, however strangely or grotesquely, as salvation for them. The situation is perilously close to that. Nevertheless, to be meaningful, Jesus *must* be (at least) *my* saviour: in that sense subjectivity has to be part of the picture. We are concerned with a *religion*, at whose heart he stands, not in the first instance a theory, which must be consistent if it is to be satisfactory.

Added to this, it has become clear how, because of his dominance in the culture, Jesus has been a focal point in many of the major developments and problems in Western intellectual and cultural history. Some of them have remained at the abstruse level of the *illuminati*, but many have come to pervade consciousness at all levels (can Christmas stories be true?). We have seen something of the sheer growth of historical knowledge and of the sharpening of historical awareness and sensitivity (What exactly happened, and what was it like?); the sense of knowledge and opinions as a human possession (*my* opinion, *my* view), of the way in which the individual or group conditions what is seen to be true; the virtual absence now of an agreed or comprehensive philosophical view of reality in which the figure of Jesus might play a part.

Jesus and the traditional beliefs about him have been much the best known focus of discussions about the role of myth in human speech and human imaging, especially when attending to the divine; that is, the virtually universal practice of speaking of the heavenly in earthly terms and in terms of the interaction of the two levels. There is the question whether and in what terms religion, and Christianity in particular, is tied to its early mythological schemes, with their angels and demons, their heavens and hells, their descents and ascensions, in particular with regard to Jesus who is an integral part of the drama in which Christianity was first couched. There seems to be here another assault on beliefs such as Jesus' pre-existence which had grown improbable on other grounds, both historical and theoretical.

Theoretical discussion of miracles has also centred on those ascribed to him or involved in his career more than on any other cases. Here, they have seemed so much more crucial, with not only history but a 'world' of belief appearing to be at stake. And discussion of the possibility or terms of divine intervention in a scientifically perceived universe finds in the incarnation a paradigm case of particular interest. Again, so much is at stake for a whole sphere of belief, about the character of the universe and about the 'freedom' of God to be himself, as well as strictly concerning Jesus. Lastly, and more recently, Jesus has become the focal point of discussion when it comes to considering the proper relationship between Christianity and other world faiths, or indeed forming an intellectual picture of the world religious scene. What exactly can be the character of the uniqueness of Jesus in such a context? It is true that the classical pattern of belief, with its exclusive claims, was elaborated in a world where Christianity competed with other faiths, not in the enclosed Christian world in which it has mostly been held. It is also true that early on Christianity found a way of accommodating that which was seen as good and true in paganism: Jesus, as pre-existent Word, had inspired it. If such an explanation now seems imperialistic as well as improbable, that may say more about the infection of Christianity by secular liberal attitudes than any error in traditional Christian claims themselves concerning Jesus' unique role. But where the 'cosmic' Jesus of the traditional pattern has faded in favour of Jesus the historical figure, then Jesus takes his place as one among numerous routes to and from the divine.

Of all these factors, none is more puzzling than the variety of beliefs about Jesus. Many of the aspects of thought and awareness just listed, where the figure of Jesus emerges as a crucial case, simply add to that diversity. Albert Schweitzer wrote with regard to the nineteenth-century 'lives' of Jesus, but his words apply more widely: 'Each individual created him in accordance with his own character. There is no historical task which so reveals a man's true self as the writing of a life of Jesus. No vital force comes into the figure unless a man breathes into it all the hate or all the love of which he is capable. The stronger the love, the stronger the hate, the more life-like is the figure produced.' In the face of such sobering thoughts, what estimate can we make of our present position?

THE MODERN TASK

Whatever the difference in their force for different people, it seems impossible that belief about Jesus should not now include some presence of the following items.

Historical perception. Whether felt as obstinate, problematic or liberating from the point of view of religious faith, the sense of Jesus as a human figure cannot now be erased from the agenda. That is not to say that he was 'just an ordinary man', with its overtones of levelling and undifferentiation. It is not even to foreclose the issue of 'unusual' events surrounding his life, though it may shift the burden of proof on to those who would claim truth for miraculous features. It is to say that he can be studied and thought of as a person constrained by a particular historical setting and by the common limitations of humankind.

This perspective or mood is bound to make the traditional story or myth concerning Jesus seem out of joint. Again, that is not to say that it may not be sustained by sophisticated argument, but, stated baldly and popularly, it becomes incredible, taking on in the modern setting of historical awareness the atmosphere of a fairy story. Historical perception cannot easily accommodate the virtually inevitable docetism (he only seemed to be human) of the old story, with its pre-existent one who came into the world for a season, only to leave it and return whence he came. Seductively and winsomely put in Christmas carols and poetry, it may draw the heart, but historical perception knows not how to contain it.

So, from this essential point of view, Jesus was a first-century Palestinian Jew, within the social and religious scene of that time and place. He may be identified (to take a selection of scholars, Jewish and Christian) as a charismatic leader (Martin Hengel), even 'the charismatic of charismatics' (Ellis Rivkin), as a transformer of Jewish categories (John Riches), or a Galilean holy man (Geza Vermes) – the differences are not crucial from the point of view of belief. They provide a framework within which belief may seek to work, perhaps a stone against which it will stumble. But where Jesus turns subtly from being the focus of faith to the creature of human ideology, then the history will be there as buffer or deflater.

Faith perception. Belief about Jesus that goes beyond mere historical assessment or admiration will work within a frame that is poles apart from that just outlined. Faith, and the beliefs in which it is expressed, tend naturally towards extravagance and exclusivity. As we saw in the case of the beginnings of faith in Jesus (p.62), their natural habitat is worship and prayer, practical 'following', and only secondarily argument and orderly statement. 'Christ our God' was Ignatius of Antioch's characteristic language at the beginning of the second century (p.59): bald, unexplained, unjustified by words. Often nowadays faith is put in undetailed terms of personal relationship. It is no wonder that when faith does seek to explain itself, whether to insiders or outsiders, the result is never wholly satisfactory, the argument never conclusive. When, in the early centuries, the medium of expression was predominantly Greek philosophy, the fit was never exact, despite the most strenuous efforts, and the best minds recognized it. There was always 'more', seen in terms of 'revelation' or the essential inaccessibility of God or the darkness meeting contemplation of God on this side of light. Perhaps the truth was not just that there was always 'more', but precisely that the fit *could* not be right, the project was flawed in attempting to conjoin two such realities.

Fitting perceptions together. Yet Greek philosophy was not short of religious possibilities. Where the lack of fit is far more apparent is when it comes to conjoining the matter and ethos of faith with historical perception in the attempt to form and state beliefs. Even so, as we saw, the attempts have been endless, and endlessly diverse. Historical perception, as an alternative to the traditional philosophical idiom of Christian belief, has tended to produce softer, more tentative, even vaguer ways of believing about Jesus: not now Jesus as the eternal Second Person of the Trinity who then took human nature; rather Jesus as the one in whom God makes himself known and available in human terms, or Jesus as the (or a?) meeting-place of divine and human, or Jesus as the human so transparent to God that in him we (best?) encounter God. Such kinds of statement seem, by comparison, hazy and inexact about 'the other world'; for good or ill, their feet are on the ground – where history happens.

All the same, it is not easy for the search for the formulation of belief to take the historical perception rounded and whole. There is often bias and selection, as if some single item or aspect were the necessary key to belief about Jesus – as when Pannenberg (*Jesus: God and Man* [London, SCM Press, 1968]) pinned so much on the resurrection, that most obscure of episodes from the historian's point of view. For some who wish to 'attend to Jesus', there is likely to be a sense of disjunction between the historical reality concerning him and making a response to him now. There may seem even more of a disjunction when the desire to respond in faith is viewed in the context of the Church, with its heritage of official faith and its heavy ecclesiasticism. In these respects sceptics and enthusiastic believers may find themselves on common ground.

There needs to be at the start a frank recognition that 'Jesus' is the acutest point in coming to terms (for yea or nay) with the Christian religion. A person may be concerned with it for all kinds of other reasons, both theoretical and practical, but the Christian faith's identity is most distinctively formed by the matter of adherence to Jesus. But there is no getting round the fact that immediately one is confronted by a Jesus who adopts different 'postures': the man of Galilee, with certain moral priorities, or with a 'cause', the kingdom of God; the crucified and/or exalted one; the one whose existence testifies to the deep involvement of God with the human race rather than his distance from it. Compatible they may be, but where among them is the emphasis to lie?

So there is no evading Jesus as riddle as well as challenge. Even if we try to confine ourselves to the purest historical perception of him, the element of riddle remains when it comes to seeking belief. The riddle is not wholly ascribable to the relative paucity of our information. Partly it is inherent in our dealings with any richly significant person, perhaps any person whatsoever. Partly it stems from our own inescapable role in the forming of our beliefs. We do not simply 'read them off' from the history, and there is no single meaning waiting to be discovered, if only we could see it. We (as individuals or members of groups or inhabitants of cultures) create meaning in our interaction with what is to be perceived. Variety is inevitable; which is not to say that 'anything goes' or that there is no scope for better and worse. Indeed, much that history tells with most assurance about Jesus restrains our tendency to create meaning that is congenial. There is discomfort in, for example, his judgements on possessions and family ties (eg. Mark 10. 17–30). There is challenge to stable values and judgements about the social order, human relations, human achievement and 'healthy' pride. In this way Jesus is like most religious leaders, with his charismatic, world-quaking character. Such people open the door to new and alarming perceptions of God.

Where is the base line? This has been written as if the source of belief (immediate once, now always mediated by inextricably complex routes) were Jesus in his first-century setting, the one we can learn to 'see' by the route of historical enquiry and imagination. We have treated that as the location of the bottom line of Christian identity. But for many that is not the case. The bottom line is the developed Christian claim, formalized with authority in AD 451 at the Council of Chalcedon, that Jesus is the 'God–Man', one person both divine and human, the essence of the classic pattern. The effect of this alternative approach is momentous for the matter of belief about Jesus, and the understanding of its significance could not be more educative for our whole subject. It means that we have before us a clearly defined pattern of belief, to be defended in its own terms or, if they are felt to be outmoded, then by using it as a basis for restatement in other terms. An example of this latter procedure is Adrian Thatcher's *Truly a Person, Truly God* (London, SPCK, 1990), described somewhat optimistically as 'a post-mythical view of Jesus'. It adopts fully the modern understanding of persons as unified beings and is therefore troubled by the artificiality (as it seems to us) of the traditional language about two natures in the one person of Jesus. Let us rather speak of two aspects or dimensions of the undoubtedly one person, analogous to the various aspects or spheres which we all know in our lives. This may certainly claim the advantage of preserving the essence of traditional belief, taking that essence to be the central assertion of Chalcedon. The implications of this procedure, and of others which seek to work from Chalcedon as base line, are of great interest. The Catholic Karl Rahner, for instance, belongs essentially to those who see the modern theological task in this way.

It is easy in the light of them to show that many modern presentations of belief about Jesus, especially those which work with a historical approach to the fore, are weak in conceptual definition. Their human Jesus moves only uncertainly towards being divine and the language fails to express his divinity with any clarity. Their Christology is 'soft' to the point of vague uncertainty. Yet these presentations, with their sights on the historical setting of Jesus and the ideas first used in the New Testament to express belief in him, must retort that if their belief is not 'hard', then neither was that of the New Testament writers. As with modern believers, those writers had no mental structure in terms of which Jesus could be described as divine in the sense that later became possible and which Chalcedon defined. They were monotheists through and through. This book has taken the view that movement in a direction that took belief away from that position began in worship and only found its eventual intellectual expression within a framework owed to Greek philosophy. So far removed is that pattern from those found in the New Testament, centring on Jesus as the apocalyptic Messiah, that Martin Werner could write of the later development as 'doctrinal fantasy' and even speak of the period in which the classic pattern was formed as one of 'unrestrained and increasing theological mendacity'! More moderately, John Ashton writes of 'the elaborate ramifications of Christian theology' which 'are precariously suspended from the metaphors' that express the Fourth Gospel's simple concentration on the *fact* of Jesus the Revealer who has come into the world.[1]

It is claimed, on the contrary, that the classic pattern did no more than bring out the implications of New Testament belief within a new framework of ideas, or develop hints within New Testament authors of whose implications they may well have been unaware. It does, however, need to be recognized how strange and blasphemous the first Christians would have found the ascription to Jesus of divinity as later conceived. Their concentration on him, and the exclusivity they ascribe to him, derive not from formal beliefs along those lines, but from his filling their horizons from end to end; from (to put it superficially) an unbounded enthusiasm which could brook no linguistic limitation just as it was limitless in its practical effects on life.

Or else appeal is made to God's providence, whereby his Church was in due course, by AD 451, led to a realization of that which earlier intellectual circumstances had made it hard to express with the necessary clarity. Or one can appeal to providence in the exercise of church authority itself. But in all these attempts, there is the oddity of assigning unique privilege to *this* moment in Christian development over all others, before and since. It may indeed be also difficult to assign such privilege (as biblically minded people often do) to the first generation of responders to Jesus, represented in the New Testament. But it is hard to see why those first responders should dance to Chalcedon's tune or be somehow constrained to affirm propositions that never occurred to them. At least, in that Jesus himself is the one about whom we seek to express belief, they bring us, however elusively, and with whatever degree of indirectness, within range of the fount of the tradition. Of course, every believer of whatever time feels an immediacy of relationship with Jesus which puts him or her on an even footing with the first responders; nevertheless, the latter open the only door(s) we have leading towards the historical figure who is one with the Jesus of present faith. Finally, while it is possible to see the 'fit' of each way of belief (from first century and from fifth) in its setting, it is another matter to speak easily of the relationship between them as one of mere re-statement or equivalence.

MOVING TO A CONCLUSION

As far back as we can trace, there have been two modes of belief about Jesus which are perhaps beyond reconciling. In the modern fascination with and endless nagging over history, one of them seems to have the pre-eminence, though the other is represented, in a fashion open to criticism for its arbitrariness, by the Chalcedon–preservers (and adapters) whose position we have been considering.

One mode is that of historical narrative. It is the mode that first appeared in the Gospels, already of course, as we saw, involving the story interpreted. (How else could we receive it and how else could it be told?) In this mode, whatever the context, the accent of belief falls on Jesus the figure of history, the actions he performed, the teaching he gave, the manner of his dying and rising; even though the *standpoint* is that of faith in the present, heavenly Jesus. Whether it is interpreted in the light of good or bad historical knowledge, here the story of Jesus is the thing. Though, in modern times, this mode has, as we have seen, tended to put the onus of proof on those making 'advanced' or formalized doctrinal claims for Jesus, it has in practice been found perfectly compatible with orthodox belief. We saw examples of that in medieval times and they could be cited from many periods. It is a mode of believing open to great variety. In recent times, for example, liberation theologies have appealed to the story of Jesus as providing the model for moral action and its validation, placing the accent on certain aspects of the story, often with relative indifference to more formal belief. Black and feminist theologies too have found it helpful to appeal to aspects of the story, to make apparent the oppression suffered by those they represent, and to authorize, indeed dictate, their struggle in the face of it. They are modern examples of a mode of believing that goes back to the evangelists themselves. There was after all no inherent compulsion on the Gospel writers to express belief about Jesus in this mode: it was the result of choice and of felt need.

The other mode is that of concept and of abstraction. Its earliest representative is Paul. Of course he was aware of Jesus as a figure of earthly history. While he may have played down, or even, in Bultmann's view, discounted outright (2 Cor. 5.16), the value of this in relation to his saving role, Jesus is not for Paul a figure whose religious importance is a balloon of speculation and ideas blown up from insignificant factual beginnings. Nevertheless, Paul tells us little of Jesus as a character in imaginable episodes or a teacher in describable contexts. To a large extent, Jesus is one acted upon more than acting: crucified by opponents, raised by God. In that sense, and despite the personal warmth in passages like Gal. 2.20, it is not misleading to describe the Jesus of Paul's writing as faceless. He is identifiable chiefly by conceptual titles like 'lord', 'son' and 'wisdom'. Attention to Jesus' life focuses chiefly on his leaving of it, in the saving acts of death and resurrection.

This tradition was continued and intensified in the 'word' Christology of the Gospel of John's prologue and of the subsequent period, in the debates and formulas of the patristic age. In so far as the emphasis fell on the divinity of Jesus, confessedly ineffable, and on his cosmic role, it was, by comparison with the Jesus of the story, still a faceless Jesus who was under discussion. So it has largely remained to this day, in the more abstract discussions of the traditional pattern of belief about him. In the context of debate and of the attempt to clarify ideas, this is wholly understandable; but there is a danger. It is that, as it were by stealth, the faceless one can come to wear unchallenged any number of faces, to suit the convictions or the convenience of those who believe in him. The emperor–Jesus of Constantine and Eusebius (p.74) is a close relation of the eternal Son who is 'of one substance with the Father' in the formula of the Council of Nicea (AD 325), in splendid simultaneity. How much of what scandalizes those who are constrained by the first mode, that of story, results from the (as it seems to them) complacent adoption of the second, that of concept? The propertied or crusading or stability seeking Church is seen to worship the orthodox Jesus of mode two, and seems to fall far short of contact with the poor, itinerant, compassionate Jesus of mode one, with his radical criticism of the rich and powerful. As is evident, traditions grow further apart the more distant they get from their source. It may now seem that between these two modes of belief (not unrelated to 'soft' and 'hard' Christologies) it is necessary to choose. Things may have gone too far for useful accommodations between the two.

There are also other choices to be made. For example, about how much weight to attach to Christian origins. We have seen that one needs argument of certain rather specialized kinds to give privilege to Chalcedon in AD 451 in the unending flow of development of Christian beliefs concerning Jesus. It is odd, to say the least, to assert the unique importance of this particular punctuation mark in history. We have also seen that while there are more straightforward reasons for attaching special significance to the first styles of belief about Jesus (their closeness in time and space to the subject of the belief, and indeed their relative simplicity and directness), these reasons are not wholly decisive, and it is possible to hold that they too have no special privilege. Insight may grow, not merely change, as Christian experience lengthens through time. But there may easily arise delusion on the part of the modern believer: we see as we cannot help seeing, we intrude into the picture of Jesus, and, as we know all too easily in the case of groups whose *idées fixes* we happen *not* to share, we easily highlight features of Jesus or angles on his life which minister to our own needs and pre-formed demands. In some measure at least, the quest for a neutral view of Jesus and of Christian origins, one fully and solely evidenced from 'the facts' (for example, from the Jewish context of his life), is a chimera.

Perhaps in any case there is more to be said for taking the present as it comes: for candidly seeing what is currently appealing or helpful about the figure of Jesus, most probably from the story, and dwelling upon it. This means frankly accepting that believing will take constantly fresh forms and that there is no resting-place. There is in this a refreshing candour. But the ghosts of Schweitzer, with his exposure of the nineteenth-century lives of Jesus the attractive liberal moralist, and of George Tyrrell with the face at the bottom of the well which is that not of Jesus but of the observer (p.8), rise up before us; and it is hard to deny that Jesus should be the critic rather than the mere endorser of those who hold beliefs about him.

This is in effect a choice about how much weight to place on the present. The Catholic Modernist of the earlier part of the present century, Alfred Loisy, and the American scholar John Knox[2] shifted weight off the historical Jesus on to the community of belief, persisting through history, which has resulted from him. It involves, theologically, a shift in the weight of belief, from belief about Jesus to belief about God or Spirit, under whom all history flows, with the episode of Jesus taking its place in the wider whole. But once more, it is hard to see much in a Christian identity which sits lightly to the disturbing presence from first-century Galilee, even if circumstances make it impossible to be faithful to much that he stood for. Disturbance may be better than complacency as the spirit in which to lead the Christian life. And, with imagination, with prayer and with Eucharist, there is ample resource for stoking the disturbance – and then for trusting it will be here and there fruitful. Christian belief without it takes some justifying.

There is no reason to suppose that the range of images forming belief about Jesus will not continue to extend in unimaginable ways. If they do not, it will be the sign that at long last Jesus has ceased to play a vital part in religious thought or indeed in reflection on life under the aura of the Christian tradition; even that he is no longer found effective for well-being with God (salvation) – which is, after all, his role![3] By the same token, the shape of the problem this occasions will remain essentially the same: concerning the criteria of genuineness and the boundaries beyond which wantonness or foolishness or misleading eccentricity dwell. One may hazard the guess that in a world where substantial bodies of people feel undervalued and oppressed, it will be the human simplicity of Jesus, playing down all human pretension and destined for death, that will occupy centre stage. It is not simply its being seen as the first of the Gospels to be written that has, after centuries of obscurity, made the Gospel of Mark the subject of intense exposition and comment, but rather the relentless pressure with which it depicts a Jesus of this character. To put it another way, whatever the forms of words, the future lies with 'soft' Christology and its natural companion, the narrative mode of belief. One may also guess that this picture of Jesus will dictate with greater force the picture of God: if God is to be credible and worshipful he must be a suffering God, not the impassible God of the traditional pattern. We have already pointed to the major break represented by this change. It reasserts from the side of the human Jesus that identity (at least in this respect) between God and Jesus which the traditional pattern of belief asserted from the divine side ('of one substance with the Father'). It ensures that Jesus is no mere formal representative of God: like the role described on the foundation stone of the Royal Coburg Theatre (now the Old Vic in south London), laid in

1816, which tells of its laying 'by His Serene Highness the Prince of Saxe Coburg and Her Royal Highness the Princess Charlotte of Wales by their Serene and Royal Highness's (*sic*) Proxy Alderman Goodbehere'. Despite the suggestion of arcane allegory in the Alderman's name, one is struck by the banality, the tenuous functional thread which links the representative to those he represents. Belief about Jesus will always seek more robust coincidences between him and God than that, whether in terms of character, objectives or 'being'. To be worth beliefs, Jesus 'shows', 'is', God to us; and belief rests on perceptions of him which chime in.

With the inevitability of proliferation of beliefs about Jesus, it is as well to keep the essence of the matter simple: in the manner of William Plomer, who, surveying images of Jesus in his poem, 'A Church in Bavaria', latched upon the strange anonymity in his having written nothing, trusting all to the air in transient spoken words, but thereby making possible a spear-sharp impact as 'a sunrise of love enlarged'.[4] That anonymity of Jesus is perhaps the single most potent fact about the origins of Christian belief in relation to later history.

There is one work from early Christianity which unites the two modes of belief we indentified earlier in this chapter: that of narrative or story and that of concept or abstraction. The Gospel of John is recognizably a version of the story of Jesus. Not only does it contain episodes from his life but it also moves forward in intelligible biographical fashion to his death. But it places the whole under the doctrine of Jesus as 'word', a faceless, non-biographical and impersonal category of understanding and belief. There have been those, indeed, notably Rudolf Bultmann, who have in effect denied the real importance of the 'story' mode as far as this Gospel is concerned. Jesus is simply 'the revealer', and there is no real content to his life or message, for all he reveals is that *he* is the revealer. But if we admit the presence of both modes in this Gospel, it is instructive to notice how much of modern discussion of it, and how much of modern difficulty in interpreting it, derive from the problem of putting the finger on the relation between the two. How important is history in fact in this Gospel? Is it abstract doctrine using history as a mere vehicle for its purposes? Or is there a fundamental concern for the story of Jesus, for Jesus as a figure in a historical story, in a real time and place, but with identifiable significance in relation to God and for human salvation?

This example illustrates something which will have struck the reader who has followed the course of this survey. It is not so much that Christian history repeats itself – while there are discernible continuities there has been constant novelty – but rather that in the telling of it the story keeps folding back upon itself. Critical methods and historical concerns that only came to light in the later parts of the story outlined in this book were in fact used already in the earlier part of our investigation. Observers and interpreters, such as ourselves, are involved in various ways in the very story which we investigate and cannot really stand back from it more than a little way; although that is a capacity to which some modern interpreters (including this one) at least aspire. No doubt a version of this aspiration moved those who first believed in Jesus in the conceptual and cosmic mode: if we can identify with him in his role above, before and beyond all things, we shall see as God sees. Too often it has proved illusory and has given the opening for the cosmic validation of all kinds of perverse as well as noble images of Jesus, most of them far removed from the Jesus of the story.

To take a leaf out of the liberationist book, perhaps the most important thing about belief in and concerning Jesus is his practical effects for life and action. We may even say that from the start much belief about him was a projection on to the heavens of plain practical effects which were traceable to him: the quality of the Christian fellowship in worship and in common life and loving care. It may be the most important thing about Jesus that he initiated such life, and the greatest betrayal of belief about him when it flags and fails, even when a great deal is being said and argued in his name. There is much to be said for just telling the story, letting be, and trusting. So the autonomously human may find a workable and life-giving relationship with the divine.

Notes

1 *The Formation of Christian Dogma* (London, A. &. C. Black, 1957), p.299; John Ashton, *Understanding the Fourth Gospel* (Oxford University Press, 1991), p.534.

2 See A. R. Vidler, *The Modernist Movement in the Roman Church* (Cambridge University Press, 1934); John Knox, *The Church and the Reality of Christ* (London, Collins, 1963).

3 This is of course the driving force behind many of the depictions of Jesus. For him to be found transformative, he must be accessible. Those puzzled or anxious about the question of how far the imaging of Jesus may properly stretch may consider feminist symbolizing of him as woman. They may then reflect whether this is any more (or less) a case of distortion than many of the other symbolizings of past and present. There is no clear reason why, if one takes a positive view of the need to re-symbolize Jesus, gender should be the one non-negotiable thread of continuity between us and the historical Jesus; why Jesus as woman should be more 'odd' than Jesus as, for example, Victorian liberal or modern freedom fighter.

4 See William Plomer, *Collected Poems* (London, Cape, 1973), p.256; and an exposition of the poem in my *Connections* (London, SCM Press, 1986), ch.11.

Further Reading

(in addition to books referred to in the text and notes)

CHAPTER 1

Don Cupitt, *The Debate about Christ* (London, SCM Press, 1979).
    A candid discussion of the many different kinds of problems raised
    by the doctrine of the incarnation of God in Christ.
John Ziesler, *The Jesus Question* (Cambridge, Lutterworth Press,
1980).
    A balanced treatment of the question of incarnation, working out
    from the New Testament.
J. S. Bowden, *Jesus – the Unanswered Questions* (London, SCM Press,
1988).
    Poses sharply a range of questions which scholarship often seems
    to evade or fudge.
R. J. Coggins and J. L. Houlden, eds, *A Dictionary of Biblical
Interpretation* (London, SCM Press, 1990).
    Contains articles on many matters of method and substance
    discussed in this book.

CHAPTER 2

John Ziesler, *Pauline Christianity* (Oxford University Press, 1983).
    A rounded introduction to Paul's teaching and issues raised by
    it.
E. P. Sanders, *Paul* (Oxford University Press, 1991).
    An account of Paul's beliefs, especially about Jesus, Israel, the
    Jewish Law and ethics.

CHAPTER 3

M. D. Hooker, *The Message of Mark* (London, Epworth Press,
1983).
    Presents the various aspects of the Gospel's teaching.
R. A. Edwards, *Matthew's Story of Jesus* (Philadelphia, Fortress,
1985).
    Brings out the flow of the message of the Gospel.
Eric Franklin, *Christ the Lord* (London, SCM Press, 1975).
    A thorough, scholarly study of Luke's teaching about Jesus.

CHAPTER 4

Martin Hengel, *The Charismatic Leader and his Followers* (Edinburgh, T. & T. Clark, 1981).

Brings out the distinctiveness of Jesus in the Judaism of his time.

Ellis Rivkin, *What Crucified Jesus?* (London, SCM Press, 1984).

Realistic historical study of the circumstances of Jesus' death.

E. P. Sanders, *Jesus and Judaism* (London, SCM Press, 1985).

Influential presentation of Jesus in the context of first-century Judaism.

G. N. Stanton, *The Gospels and Jesus* (Oxford University Press, 1989).

A dependable treatment of Jesus in history and as presented in the Gospels, and the relation between them.

John Riches, *The World of Jesus* (Cambridge University Press, 1991).

A picture of the background of Jesus' life. (Relates also to ch.3.)

CHAPTER 5

James D. G. Dunn, *Christology in the Making* (London, SCM Press, 1980).

An account of the development of belief in Jesus observable in the New Testament.

CHAPTER 6

M. F. Wiles, *The Making of Christian Doctrine* (Cambridge University Press, 1974).

Discusses the emergence of theology in the early centuries of the Church.

R. A. Markus, *Christianity in the Roman World* (London, Thames & Hudson, 1974).

Perceptive presentation of early Christianity, showing the context of early beliefs in the world of the period.

R. P. C. Hanson, *The Search for the Christian Doctrine of God* (Edinburgh, T. & T. Clark, 1988).

Full treatment of the development of the classic formulation of doctrine about Jesus in relation to God.

CHAPTER 7

R. W. Southern, *The Making of the Middle Ages* (London, Cresset Library, 1987).

Contains material on the changes of sensibility in relation to Jesus during the early medieval period.

Colin Morris, *The Discovery of the Individual 1050–1200* (London, SPCK, 1972).

Shows the setting in which medieval belief took shape.

Miri Rubin, *Corpus Christi, the Eucharist in Late Medieval Culture* (Cambridge University Press, 1991).

Describes the vastly important and pervasive role of the eucharist in focusing and expressing belief about Jesus, especially in the Middle Ages.

CHAPTER 8

M. F. Wiles, *The Remaking of Christian Doctrine* (London, SCM Press, 1974).

Shows how the classic pattern of doctrine now needs to be reformulated in the light of modern understanding.

Keith W. Clements, *Lovers of Discord* (London, SPCK, 1988).

A historical account of the numerous debates, mostly on belief about Jesus, in English Christianity in the past 150 years and more.

John Macquarrie, *Jesus Christ in Modern Thought* (London, SCM Press, 1990).

A full-scale account of theological treatment of Jesus throughout the centuries, with suggestions for modern understanding.

CHAPTER 9

J. L. Houlden, *Connections* (London, SCM Press, 1986).

Discusses the problems raised for belief by modern study of the New Testament.

Ruth Page, *The Incarnation of Freedom and Love* (London, SCM Press, 1991).

An attempt to look afresh at Christology in the light of current questions. It may be seen as a complement to *this* book, approaching the subject from a more conceptual standpoint.

Sarah Coakley, *Christ Without Absolutes* (Oxford University Press, 1988).

The latter part of this book in particular serves as an excellent reflection on some of the issues discussed in my chapters 8 & 9, by way of a study of the many-sided thought of Ernst Troeltsch (whom I have not used as an example).

Index of Names and Subjects

Index of Biblical References